PRAISE FOR

IN-LAWS, OUTLAWS
AND THE
FUNCTIONAL FAMILY

Harry is an extraordinary man who has written an extraordinary book, which I believe will be used by the Lord as a catalyst to heal and strengthen the family. I highly recommend this outstanding book!

CHÉ AHN
SENIOR PASTOR, HARVEST ROCK CHURCH
PASADENA, CALIFORNIA

Bishop Harry Jackson is an emerging leader in the Body of Christ. He is among the intellectually astute, but he also has spiritual depth. Of the things written in this book, he goes from precept to practice and there is a restorative effect for the culture in the principles written here. He is a new generation resource man and I highly commend his writing and teaching. I say, unequivocally, that he is a man of God.

BISHOP WELLINGTON BOONE
AUTHOR, *YOUR WIFE IS NOT YOUR MOMMA: HOW YOU CAN HAVE HEAVEN IN YOUR HOME*
ATLANTA, GEORGIA

Bishop Harry Jackson's book *In-Laws, Outlaws and the Functional Family* is a valuable tool needed by every Christian parent. It quickly becomes apparent that he is not writing a book of theory. As a pastor and parent, he has "been there, done that." He is extremely candid in his personal illustrations, and this transparency makes the book both very readable and extremely believable. As the spiritual father of Bishop Harry Jackson, I can honestly declare that the many personal illustrations he uses in this book are true to his life and are applicable to our lives. The principles expounded here have worked for him; why wouldn't they work for the rest of us?

DR. JUDSON CORNWALL
PASTOR, TEACHER, AUTHOR
PHOENIX, ARIZONA

Bishop Jackson combines revelation, practical teaching and humor in his wonderful book. He provides us with powerful answers that everyone can use. I highly recommend it.

FRANCIS FRANGIPANE
AUTHOR AND PASTOR, RIVER OF LIFE MINISTRIES
CEDAR RAPIDS, IOWA

In a society that undermines the idea of marriage for life and the development of biblical virtues in children, Bishop Harry Jackson has provided wise, down-to-earth counsel based on solid scriptural principles for safekeeping family relationships. I highly recommend *In-Laws, Outlaws and the Functional Family*.

DUTCH SHEETS
AUTHOR, *INTERCESSORY PRAYER* AND *TELL YOUR HEART TO BEAT AGAIN*
SENIOR PASTOR, SPRINGS HARVEST FELLOWSHIP
COLORADO SPRINGS, COLORADO

In-Laws, Outlaws and the Functional Family guides us through all the drama and confusion that keeps families struggling and divided. Harry Jackson writes with the authority of a seasoned leader, the guidance of a concerned father, the passion of a loving husband and the wisdom of one who has experienced what he has written about. This book is informative, challenging, empowering—and fun!

ALVIN SLAUGHTER
PRESIDENT AND FOUNDER, ALVIN SLAUGHTER INTERNATIONAL
WARWICK, NEW YORK

Bishop Harry R. Jackson, Jr., has a Harvard MBA; he is a pastor; he is a teacher. His weekly television program is broadcast internationally. He has a radio program. But more important than all of these efforts and achievements, Harry Jackson, Jr., is a husband and a father. He is committed to creating homes where "God is exalted and the family is protected." You will find *In-Laws, Outlaws and the Functional Family* to be what it bills itself to be—"A Real-World Guide to Resolving Family Issues." From "It's A Jungle in Here" to the final "Out of the Jungle"—this book is quite a safari of information through the issues that face today's family. You won't be disappointed when you practice what he preaches!

TOMMY TENNEY
AUTHOR, *THE GOD CHASERS*
PRESIDENT AND FOUNDER, GODCHASERS.NETWORK

Harry Jackson has ministered at our church on many occasions. He is always very well received because of his honest heart and his practical yet spiritual approach in dealing with issues that touch us where we all live. These characteristics have come through in the book you are about to read. The illustrations from history, his years of experience as a pastor, as well as his candidness in his own struggles make this valuable reading. The war for the family is being waged not only in America but throughout the world. May God use this book to aid in bringing forth functional families that will exemplify the love, wisdom and power of God's kingdom to a world that is in great need of such a demonstration.

COLIN URQUHART
SENIOR PASTOR, KINGDOM FAITH CHURCH
HORSHAM, ENGLAND

IN-LAWS
OUTLAWS
AND THE
Functional
FAMILY

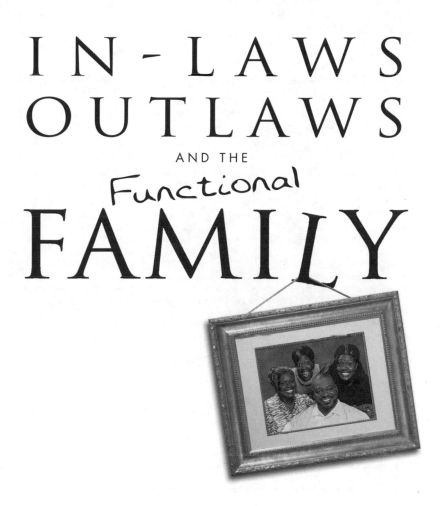

DR. HARRY R. JACKSON, JR.

Regal

From Gospel Light
Ventura, California, U.S.A.

Published by Regal Books
From Gospel Light
Ventura, California, U.S.A.
Printed in the U.S.A.

Regal Books is a ministry of Gospel Light, an evangelical Christian publisher dedicated to serving the local church. We believe God's vision for Gospel Light is to provide church leaders with biblical, user-friendly materials that will help them evangelize, disciple and minister to children, youth and families.

It is our prayer that this Regal book will help you discover biblical truth for your own life and help you meet the needs of others. May God richly bless you.

For a free catalog of resources from Regal Books/Gospel Light, please call your Christian supplier or contact us at 1-800-4-GOSPEL *or* www.regalbooks.com.

Cover and interior design by Robert Williams
Edited by Keith Wall and Amy Simpson
Editorial Assistant: Kathryn T. Schuh
Cover Photo by Tom Radcliffe, Point of View Studio

Library of Congress Cataloging-in-Publication Data
Jackson, Harry R.
    In-laws, outlaws and the functional family / Harry R. Jackson.
        p. cm.
    Includes bibliographical references.
        ISBN 0-8307-2967-4
    1. Family—Religious life.   I. Title.
    BV4526.2 .J33 2002
    248.4—dc21   2002010846

1 2 3 4 5 6 7 8 9 10 11 12 13 14 15 / 09 08 07 06 05 04 03 02

Rights for publishing this book in other languages are contracted by Gospel Light Worldwide, the international nonprofit ministry of Gospel Light. Gospel Light Worldwide also provides publishing and technical assistance to international publishers dedicated to producing Sunday School and Vacation Bible School curricula and books in the languages of the world. For additional information, visit www.gospellightworldwide.org; write to Gospel Light Worldwide, P.O. Box 3875, Ventura, CA 93006; or send an e-mail to info@gospellightworldwide.org.

DEDICATION

This book is lovingly dedicated to my father, Harry R. Jackson, Sr.
Despite his untimely death when I was 22 years old, his pithy
statements and axioms have been guiding lights to me throughout
my life. The concepts expressed in this book are basically an
updated version of many of his beliefs mixed with
biblical principles and research.

My dad was a giant in love and commitment to his family.
He impacted my mother, my brother, Eric, and myself with an
empowering love that has been a source of strength for all of us
to this day. Whenever I think of him, I see his affirming smile
and I hear an exhortation based on Philippians 4:13:
You can do all things through Christ, who strengthens you.

Contents

FOREWORD

Movies and television programs depict families of all types: lesbian families, gay-male families, single-parent families, multigenerational families, grandparent-as-parent families, blended-household families and occasionally even traditional families. Behavioral studies proclaim the decline in marriage, the rise in cohabitation, the rapid escalation of children born outside of marital relationships and the continuation of divorce as the norm. Attitudinal studies show the conflict between young people's hopes of having a lasting marriage and their doubt that it's possible. Counselors recount tale after tale of errant assumptions, unreasonable expectations and aberrant sexual behavior among couples. Pastors bemoan the difficulty of striving to convince people that the Bible has principles relevant to their marriage and family life. Liberal state and local governments are regularly addressing the possibility of recognizing gay and lesbian liaisons as the modern family norm.

Indisputably, the public's notion of family is less certain than ever before. The incredible challenges raised by the prevalence of postmodern thinking and behavior in our society raise a pertinent and critical question: Does the family matter anymore?

I suppose that question is the subject matter for a book of its own—one that as recently as two decades ago we might have argued was completely unnecessary. But that question is as germane as the answer is obvious: Yes, the family is incredibly significant and it matters more than most people realize.

WHY DOES FAMILY MATTER?

God Tells Us of Its Importance

The Bible is replete with stories about relationships. Some of the most important relationships and teachings about relationships concern family. Scripture teaches that family is one of God's primary mechanisms for preparing us for and enabling us to maximize life on Earth. What God esteems, we ought to cherish.

It Is One of the Primary Means Through Which We Experience, Interpret and Respond to an Invasive, Elusive and Soul-Threatening Culture

We are influenced by our environment. In America, pop culture impacts who we are in enormous ways. In fact, the cultural forces we experience every day are too pervasive, powerful, dynamic and complex for any individual to understand and manage without substantial assistance and support. The family—in its three primary forms (nuclear, extended and church)—is God's mechanism for helping each of us maneuver through cultural complexities to become healthy and whole persons, fervent disciples of Christ and solid representatives of His kingdom.

It Is the Primary Place Through Which Moral Development Must Be Nurtured

Sadly, many families abdicate their responsibility for the moral, ethical and spiritual development of their children, allowing the media and social institutions to assume that role. God's intention was that parents guide their children through the maze of moral alternatives to embrace and live out a biblical worldview.

When families abandon this fundamental duty, they tacitly accept moral defeat. Contrary to popular thought, it does not take a village to raise a child; it takes a mother and a father committed to God's truth and His principles for living to shape a life into something that honors Him and reflects His goodness. The community in which that family lives may assist in the process or, more commonly in America these days, the community may provide the undoing of what the family has tried so hard to inculcate in its young ones. In a hyper-tolerant culture, allowing the village to raise a person creates a human being with lowest-common-denominator values and morals—a child of compromise, convenience and consensus. God calls on parents to use the family environment and resources to raise up champions of His faith and values.

It Is Parents and Siblings Who Have the Greatest Impact on Our Notions of Deity, Understanding of Sin and Choice Regarding Spiritual Salvation
Our research shows that our religious journey is uniquely personal but greatly influenced by those whom we love and, in most cases, that is (or should be) our family. A noteworthy correlation exists between a parent who has embraced Christ as his or her Savior and the propensity of their children to do likewise.

WHAT WILL IT TAKE?

Family matters. But its significance does not mask the fact that America's families are under siege and many are losing the battle. What, then, will it take for families to be stronger and healthier?

There is no single answer to this sweeping question, but one of the most common replies people offer is "Our church is responsible for building up our family and helping it to stay strong." Many may endorse this idea, but it is not primarily the church's duty to stabilize and fortify families. It is our personal responsibility to do so, with guidance, support and encouragement from our church. My research shows that all too often Americans place the responsibility for family development on the shoulders of individuals or organizations who can help, but they fail to realize that those entities will not make a family what it ultimately becomes. You and I must accept that God-given responsibility as our primary obligation as well as the consequences of our family-related choices.

Perhaps the most unequivocal answer we can provide is that it takes each individual accepting personal responsibility to do whatever he or she can do to facilitate a healthy family. Therefore, the first step in creating a healthy family is to embrace our roles and responsibilities in the process.

If you are at all like me, though, this recognition sends a shock wave of fear rippling through your body. Even now that little voice inside my head is yelling out, *I don't know all the answers. I'm not sure I can handle all of this. In fact, I didn't really know what I was getting myself into when I got married, when I had my first child, when . . .* The bottom line: being responsible for a family can be terrifying. Most of us are constantly seeking new sources of wisdom and help in our effort to be the best spouse, parent and family member possible.

Fortunately, there are some very capable individuals who are a step or two ahead of us on the journey to fostering a functional family. Harry Jackson is one of those shining lights. He is a bright, passionate strategic leader being used by God to help shape and sharpen the lives of thousands of people. As you read this book, you will quickly discover that Bishop Jackson is not merely content to recite the litany of statistics describing the challenges facing families and to generically encourage us to do something about the morass. He is skilled at providing practical ways of perceiving and handling those challenges. Within these pages, you will encounter a helpful road map to guide you and your family to a more fulfilling and God-honoring place.

Perhaps the breadth of subject matter addressed in this book will surprise you. The bishop tackles family roles, communication, conflict, parenting, sexuality, finances, relatives—all the things that we hate to talk about openly but that miff us in private. The range of insights provided arms you with a virtual handbook of family assistance, a resource that examines the very issues that you and I are likely to confront, without warning, on any given day.

Using his life and ministry as a source of personal insight, Bishop Jackson provides down-to-earth examples and ideas for our consideration. These days, Americans are most likely to change their behavior after they have seen an alternative modeled by others whom they know and trust. I bet that before you're done reading this book, you will feel as if you know Harry, Michele, Joni and Elizabeth Jackson well enough to trust that their victories over life's challenges—and the lessons they have learned from efforts that did not pan out as planned—can help you with similar battles in your life. When seeking a family to observe for clues to a healthy family life, I'd take the Jacksons over the Osbournes any day!

FINAL THOUGHT

This book should come with a warning label on the front cover, something like "Danger: Change Required. See Inside for Details." If you are *not* ready to engage in some serious self-assessment, to alter some of your existing behaviors and attitudes, and to trust God's principles and power, then this book is not for you. But if you *are* willing to take a look at who you really are and what you do, and to align your heart with God's—

allowing your thoughts and actions to follow—then you will find many pearls of wisdom embedded in these pages.

The family matters. I pray that Bishop Jackson's prescriptions for family health will be just the medicine you need to handle the family challenges you are facing or will face.

George Barna
Directing Leader, Barna Research Group, Ltd.
Ventura, California

ACKNOWLEDGMENTS

Finishing this book is certainly a dream come true. First of all, I thank God for the awesome privilege of sharing His Word and helpful hints to the thousands who will read this book. Next, there are many "earthly beings" who have invested a great deal in the development of this project. I want to acknowledge as many of them as I can. The entire book is a celebration of my love for the former Vivian Michele Alexander and the two beautiful daughters she gave me, Joni and Elizabeth. Thank you all for your untiring commitment to me! Yet special acknowledgment needs to be made to Elizabeth, who endured a week with Dad by herself as we worked through the rigors of exams, her spring musical review, manuscript deadlines and Mom's absence because of a missions trip.

To Essie Jackson, my mom, "I thank my God every time I remember you" (Phil. 1:3). Your prayers have been a part of God's life-support system for me my entire life. Ironically, just as you gave birth to me with hard labor in the natural, you have also helped birth this book in a similar manner. A special word of thanks must also be given to Dr. Judson Cornwall, my spiritual father. My commitment to writing is largely due to your example and encouragement. Thank you for being there in my darkest moments of ministry and rejoicing with me over victories others would not understand. You are a champion and my spiritual hero.

To all my friends at Regal, thanks for believing in me and coaching me through this arduous process. Bill Greig III, you saw a diamond in the rough in the Family at War audiocassette series and made a commitment to bring forth its beauty. Kyle Duncan, I felt a sense of connection with you from our first meeting. Your wisdom and creativity have provided me clear guidance all the way. Deena Davis, I will never forget the encouraging conversations with you as we trudged through the rewriting process. You helped me see the big picture. Keith Wall, my editor, your comments and coaching have helped me more than words can express. I know that the warfare has been severe, but you've been a true soldier of the Cross. Thanks for your vigilant care for this project.

Now, let's talk about the Hope Christian Church family. To Jan Sherman, who spent countless hours overseeing the transcription of audiocassettes, organizing and editing rough drafts, directing research and performing countless other duties not previously included in her job description. Without you, there would be no book. A special thanks to Deacon Oliver Foxe, who served the entire writing and research team with your patient attention to our logistical needs. Marcille Moss, Tyra Holland, Tracy Everette, Christine McGruder and Delores Camphor, you all made invaluable contributions to research, editing and typing. Also a special thanks to Rev. Lillie Jackson and Tina Green from our counseling and personal ministry department at Hope Christian Church. You not only have helped thousands of people over the years, but also have helped me remain in touch with our congregation's current needs. This book will serve as a tool for your ongoing leadership training. Last, but not least, I want to thank the elders and congregation of Hope Christian Church for their love, prayers and support, which made this book a "corporate" work.

CHAPTER 1

IT'S A JUNGLE IN HERE!

The Family Is at War

It is fatal to enter any war without the will to win it.

Douglas MacArthur, at the 1952 Republican National Convention

In 1455, two combat-ready armies approached a place called St. Albans in England. They were initiating a power struggle that would affect much of the world—especially England—and reverberate through history. Ironically, the soldiers who marched toward battle were acquaintances. In fact, the armies represented two branches of the same family. The conflict would come to be known as the War of the Roses.

This war was so named because the two families—or houses—that fought had a rose as part of their coats of arms. One family had a red rose, which was the symbol of the House of Lancaster, led by Queen Margaret of Anjou and Cardinal Edmund Beaufort, who joined forces in an alliance of power. The other family's symbol was a white rose, which was held by Richard, Duke of York, who vied for the throne. Shakespeare would later dramatize this man as an uncaring, immoral opportunist who would kill even his family if it served his needs.

The rose is a symbol of romantic love; it symbolizes fidelity, beauty and faithfulness. But in the hands of the two warring family factions the rose represented treachery, infidelity and an insatiable hunger for power. How had the family deteriorated into two contentious and vengeful factions? What brought people who should have loved one another to the point of blood lust and brutality?

It is the same reason that we kill our contemporary marriages. How is it that we start with two beautiful people, two vibrant roses, and end up with a jungle of a relationship that ends in physical or emotional war? The English families of the War of the Roses were not facing an external enemy. Instead, they were locked into mortal combat fueled by internal strife. Let's look at how this powerful family turned so sour, paying attention to how to avoid their tragic mistakes.

It began with Edward III, who was coronated nearly 128 years before the war. His father had brought the reputation of the English throne to its nadir before his death. Edward II had been murdered by English nobles, partly because they reviled his bisexual lifestyle. Young Edward was only 14 years old when he assumed the throne of England.[1]

During his early days, Edward III reached out to other monarchs in Europe. He specifically attempted to make peace with France, but they felt that he was ill-mannered and had not fully submitted himself to the French monarch. From that moment on, Edward's life seemed to be marked with a desire to prove himself and his nation to the world. He carried a macho attitude to the extreme. And since his father had brought shame upon the family line through unmanly behavior, Edward wanted to be known as a man's man.

His wife endured his absences and many affairs, which were part of a warring king's lifestyle. Edward's sons later despised the military-like upbringing they received. Edward played favorites and even designated his grandson, a child of his favorite boy, as heir to throne. If only Edward had been able to answer four questions, England would have been spared one of the most divisive civil wars of history. Answering these questions would also help resolve strife and war in the modern-day home.

1. How do we stop power struggles within our marriages?
2. How can we raise each of our children with a sense of personal destiny?
3. How do we develop strong values and principles in our children's lives?
4. What are the keys to helping women and our daughters use their unique influence to promote godliness?

BACK TO BASICS

Is it an overstatement to say there's a war being waged for families in America and around the world today? Is it only an exaggeration to suggest that a battle is raging for the survival of the *institution* of the family as well as millions of *individual* families? No, it is not, because you know the truth. You know, as I do, that families are in desperate trouble. I could fill these pages with grim statistics about divorce rates, family breakdown, infidelity and domestic violence. Let me mention just a few.

- According to the U.S. Census Bureau, approximately half of all first marriages that begin this year will end in divorce.[2]
- A 1998 Census Bureau report showed that the number of divorced people more than quadrupled between 1970 and 1996.[3]
- A 1999 study by researchers at Rutgers University found that only 25 percent of all marriages that began 10 years ago are "enduring and happy." In other words, three-fourths of all couples who were wed a decade ago are now either divorced or still together but unhappily.[4]

Some Christians may rationalize away such statistics by saying, "People of faith and strong religious commitment surely don't divorce *that* much." Tragically, that's not the case. Respected researcher George Barna recently released a study showing that the divorce rates among Christians are *higher* than the general population.

There's no doubt that marital breakdown affects every segment of society—Christian and non-Christian, young and old, rich and poor, educated and uneducated. Both ministers and movie stars are experiencing divorce. Christian leaders and corporate executives, gospel singers and rock musicians all see their marriages dissolve. Yes, millions of men and women end their marriages each year, and even more languish in miserable relationships.[5]

Despite all this, people still want to get married. Little girls still dream of their wedding day and the fulfillment of having children. Men still long to find the woman who will be a lover and a friend. Single people still long for a soul mate, a lifelong companion who will know them and accept them at the deepest level. Somehow God's plan for one woman and one man together for a lifetime still appeals to us. We want to be loved, we want to be happy, we want to travel through life with a loyal partner.

> We want to be loved, we want to be happy, we want to travel through life with a loyal partner.

Who, then, has the solution to these vexing problems? How can we bridge the gap between dreams and reality? How can we keep our homes together and live in harmony as God intended?

ARISE TO THE OCCASION

Because of the enormity of the problems facing marriages and families, we need radical solutions. And that is what I intend to offer in the following pages. But before you get ahead of me, I must explain the kinds of remedies I'll propose. We often use the word "radical" to describe something way out there, revolutionary or avant-garde. Contrary to popular belief, "radical" literally means "to return to the roots."[6] So the only hope for the institution of marriage is reaffirming the bedrock, enduring Christian values.

As a former football player, I know that when things aren't going well on the field, when teams aren't winning, coaches go back to basics. "We've got to relearn the fundamentals, all the rudimentary skills that will lead to success," coaches say. And so, too, must we if we're going to help marriages thrive and flourish.

We need to return to the essentials in order to withstand the forces that seek to erode the stability of our families.

Even as we embrace the long-established biblical fundamentals, we must be culturally relevant, understanding the unique challenges of our times. Though marriages in every era have experienced difficulties and dilemmas, the pressures exerted by our present-day society can seem overwhelming. We must address today's timely complexities with timeless counsel—the guiding principles handed down by God Himself.

> **We need to return to the essentials in order to withstand the forces that seek to erode the stability of our families.**

A few months ago I received a phone call from a woman who had to flee with her children from a violent husband. Those precious little ones had been battered by the man who had vowed to love, honor and protect their mother. I was surprised and dismayed to learn this, since the father had appeared to be a decent, committed family man. But like so many people, this family had lived in quiet pain for years.

It turns out that the father had become distraught over dire financial struggles, and he began drinking heavily. Soon his craving for alcohol dominated his life, and he developed a serious problem. Sam began hanging around with drinking buddies, a rough crowd who encouraged his irresponsible behavior. It wasn't long before one bad choice—numbing his pain with booze—led to more bad choices. He began shoplifting and stealing from coworkers. And he began gambling away what little money he had. With his behavior and attitude spiraling downward, he ended up taking out his frustrations on his family in violent fits of rage.

Clearly a war was taking place within Sam's heart and soul. He was losing the battle and—in the process—losing his family.

It's tempting to think that nothing like this will ever happen to you. Maybe you'll never struggle with alcohol addiction, theft or domestic violence; but you may struggle with lying, anger or bitterness. Perhaps the battle you'll fight will be against arrogance, pride or selfishness. No sin is too small for the enemy to use to divide families. The truth is that all of our marriages are at war. If we are not fighting with each other, then we are fighting with a culture that tears at the very fabric of our homes.

As we assess the condition of the family in our society, we have to wonder whether the family as we know it can succeed. In the inner cities, fatherless homes have become the majority, while suburbs are filled with a growing number of angry children who have become perverted by privilege.[7] The recent rash of mothers who kill their own children has caused alarm in both the Church and the psychiatric communities.

The famed anthropologist Margaret Mead said, "In every known society, we find some form of the family."[8] As time progressed she later declared, "We must find a substitute for the family."[9] Unfortunately, many people are indeed finding substitute families. Gangs like the Bloods and the Crips have become substitute families for some urban youth.[10] Internet chat rooms are replacing living rooms as places to exchange ideas and share feelings. Millions of unmarried couples choose to cohabitate, or "live together," forming quasi families that remain committed as long as the partners are happy but dissolve as soon as things turn sour. Surely traditional marriage is in danger of becoming extinct.

Therefore, it is time for each of us to face our personal problems and thereby address the problems of our culture. Individuals who are willing to go to battle can become part of a grassroots war against the forces that challenge our families. Abraham Lincoln, in reference to fighting problems, said, "The occasion is piled high with difficulty, but we must arise to the occasion."[11]Arising to this occasion puts us in a position to receive God's power in order to solidify our marriages and families.

GUIDANCE AT OUR FINGERTIPS

Most people reach moments in their lives in which the future seems uncertain, when the path ahead is unclear. Even the most confident of us have been hit by setbacks outside of our control. Sudden economic downturns, unfriendly in-laws, illnesses, crises with children and toxic internal family practices threaten our future. At times like these, we need help. We must be humble enough to receive assistance—and courageous enough to ask for it.

One night I was on my way to appear on a live radio program at a station in northern Virginia. I had traveled along the Potomac River before in daylight with absolutely no problem. I had left in plenty of time to get settled and prepare myself to encourage the listening audience. Or so I thought. When I took a wrong turn, I began to drive in unfamiliar territory. I called the station and warned the producer that I would be late. Then I continued to drive around in circles, and more circles and more circles.

I never made it to the station that night. The producer was forced to air a previously recorded program, and I went home disappointed and chagrined. I was too proud to stop and ask for directions.

My twilight wanderings are similar to what happens in many of our marriages and families. We know where we want to go. We know our destination. But we simply get confused and lost in the darkness. Often our pride keeps us from asking for the help we really need. If you are tired of meaningless skirmishes with the enemy and wandering around in the darkness, this book may be your first step toward victorious Christian living.

In my 20 years of pastoral ministry, I have seen God's power manifest itself again and again in honor to the Word of God. Although the family is at war, God's Word still helps us win life's battles. It seems that the Lord delights in confounding the wisdom of the world. He can heal and restore situations that we think are hopeless.

God at Work

A few years ago an elder of a disbanding church came to me with a dilemma. He had left one disappointing situation and unwittingly entered another. He had just started attending a church in which the leader had been involved in a homosexual affair years before. The elder described his family's delight with the new church and their conviction to follow God's leading, but he was concerned about the minister's past. So I asked the elder if he thought Jesus still sets the captive free. My next statement stunned this prominent church leader: If God's power will not work for this pastor, then perhaps it won't work for anyone, including you and me.

I reminded him that we all have past failures we'd just as soon forget. In fact, the apostle Paul concludes an amazing list of sins by saying, "And such were some of you" (1 Cor. 6:11, NKJV).

The elder thought for a moment and then said, "But what if he falls again?"

I said, "We simply have to trust that the same God who keeps us on the straight and narrow will guide and protect the pastor as well."

After much prayer, the elder chose to stay in the church, and his family has thrived within this body. Thankfully, the pastor has proved to be a godly man and has not fallen back into his homosexual lifestyle.

Do we really believe that "the LORD sets prisoners free" (Ps. 146:7)? Do we believe that He can do "immeasurably more than all we ask or imagine" (Eph. 3:20)? Do we believe Jesus' words when He said, "Anyone who has faith in me will do what I have been doing. He will do even greater things than these" (John 14:12)? How we respond to these questions will largely determine whether we'll trudge along in mediocre marriages or enjoy magnificent ones.

VICTORY ON THE HORIZON

Please hear the message of my heart. I write these words as a "wounded healer"—one who has faced the same struggles, challenges and temptations as every married person. For several years, I worked as a national sales manager for a Fortune 500 company, and I allowed my career pursuits to undermine my family life. What's more, my wife, Michele, and I have had to address and overcome unhealthy patterns and behaviors we carried into marriage. We've worked through many painful issues that could have easily destroyed our relationship.

As I reflect on my own marriage, I think of the words in 2 Corinthians 1:3-4:

> Praise be to the God and Father of our Lord Jesus Christ . . . who comforts us in all our troubles, so that we can comfort those in any trouble with the comfort we ourselves have received from God.

That's the spirit in which I write—a fellow traveler endeavoring to pass along the comfort and wisdom I've received from the Lord.

What I've learned in my own marriage and in two decades of ministry is that Jesus can mend any broken relationship. He wants to guide you into His greatest blessings. He's done it for me, and He can do it for you. Is it tough to maintain a healthy, happy marriage year after year? You bet it is! Is it hard to "hang in there" when the easiest thing seems to be walking away from the hassles and heartaches? Absolutely! But let me share some good news with you.

> You are a chosen people, a royal priesthood, a holy nation, a people belonging to God, that you may declare the praises of him who called you out of darkness into his wonderful light (1 Pet. 2:9).

There is no reason to have a defeatist, pessimistic, gloomy attitude toward marriage. There is no reason you should entertain thoughts about giving up or throwing in the towel. If you are a Christian, God has called you—yes, *you*—to reflect His glory. God wants to do a mighty work of restoration in your life that will reflect His awesome nature. Restoration of broken marriages and hurting families is possible because of the transforming power of God's mercy.

Perhaps my thoughts are best summarized by the words of J. Allan Petersen, who said, "There have to be sufficient spiritual resources in Jesus Christ to enable parents and children to succeed in this day—or else Christianity is a hoax. It is an impractical philosophy—something for the hot house instead of the open road—that thrives only under ideal conditions which never exist."[12]

We can experience true victory when we walk in the Word. Our marriages and families can be living testimonies to the abundant life and eternal joy God promises His children. We can indeed enjoy peace and harmony instead of war and strife.

CHAPTER 2

To Be or Not to Be an Awesome Couple?

Maximizing God's Glory in Marriage

Marriage is like the army. Everyone complains, but you'd be surprised at how many reenlist.

Anonymous

Picture this: God brings you and your spouse together, and you know it was a "match made in heaven." You're soul mates, best friends and passionate lovers. You and your partner are in an eternal state of romantic love, and your interactions are tender and supportive. Even as you work your way through tedious daily chores, you have ample time to enjoy each other and your children. A spirit of camaraderie and teamwork pervades your household. Disagreements are handled easily in a tolerant, constructive manner. You hurry home from work each evening, eager to return to your loved ones and the shelter they provide. Then each night, as you drift off into peaceful sleep, you think, *How did I get so blessed? Thank you, God, for blessing me so richly.*

Is this scenario fantasy or reality? Is it fact or fiction? Am I being serious or sarcastic?

It's true that life on Earth will never be perfect. There will always be headaches and hassles, aggravations and annoyances. Because we're human, we'll always have conflicts and squabbles. Nevertheless, there are times I honestly experience the sense of joy and delight captured in the vignette above. There have even been entire weeks in which my feet almost never touched the ground. (That's quite a feat for a 250-pound ex-football player!)

Celebrating my 25th wedding anniversary not long ago, I was reminded once again that I married the right woman. In God's unfailing love and mercy, my life has been enriched by my relationship with a woman who has walked with me through both my greatest achievements and darkest moments. Michele is my friend, lover, partner and confidante.

Marriage should have the loving commitment, mutual support, passionate excitement and close camaraderie depicted in the great love stories of literature and film. Call me an incurable romantic, but I believe our homes can be filled with incredible joy, where marriages bring tremendous satisfaction. Indeed, a careful study of the Bible reveals that the Lord inaugurated a twofold mission for the family:

1. To be a place of fulfillment for husband and wife.
2. To be a place where God's glory and character are revealed.

God desires that our families become an advertisement for His kingdom and His character. He wants our marriages to be living, breathing, public-service announcements declaring the brilliance of His plan for mankind. The Lord will indeed supply our families with all of heaven's resources if we earnestly endeavor to follow God's will.

> God wants our marriages to be living, breathing, public-service announcements declaring the brilliance of His plan for mankind.

Hear what the writer of Revelation says:

Let us rejoice and be glad and give him glory! For the wedding of the Lamb has come, and his bride has made herself ready. Fine linen, bright and clean, was given her to wear (19:7-8).

Christ's "marriage" to His Church serves as a model for our earthly unions, which should be overflowing with joy, gladness and celebration. The fine garments referred to represent the righteousness of the saints. These clothes are indicative of the character and lifestyle choices we must make to ensure true joy in our marriages.

THE HEART OF THE MATTER

You and your spouse have a choice to be either a great, God-honoring couple or an average, mediocre one. You decide each day whether you will run the race in such a way as to get the prize (see 1 Cor. 9:24) or limp along in a halfhearted effort. You resolve to make your home a place of joy and laughter or boredom and apathy. William Jennings Bryan could have been speaking of marriage when he said, "Destiny is not a matter of chance, it is a matter of choice. It is not a thing to be waited for, it is a thing to be achieved."[1] The difference between awesome couples and average ones is determination—the decision to pursue greatness or settle for mediocrity.

The theme of choice and how we decide to live is woven throughout the Bible.

> Then choose for yourselves this day whom you will serve (Josh. 24:15).

> Choose my instruction instead of silver, knowledge rather than choice gold (Prov. 8:10).

> If anyone chooses to do God's will, he will find out whether my teaching comes from God or whether I speak on my own (John 7:17).

Clearly from the Scriptures, God gives us the free will to make choices that affect the quality of our lives, including our marriages. Though He stands ready to empower us with His strength and resources, it's up to us to take the first step and ask for God's help.

> Ask and it will be given to you; seek and you will find; knock and the door will be opened to you. For everyone who asks receives; he who seeks finds; and to him who knocks, the door will be opened (Matt. 7:7-8).

DIFFERENT PERSPECTIVES

Our society is deeply ambivalent about marriage. Some people applaud marriage while others scoff, and some people both applaud and scoff at the same time. Many people approach marriage as though it will be the answer to all their problems. Other people sense it's time to get married but do so reluctantly. A great number of men and women want the freedom of singleness along with the benefits of marriage. What seems to be the ideal for many would be an open marriage. Some time ago, Sarah Ferguson, the Duchess of York, appeared on the *Larry King Live* show, where she described the unique relationship she had with her ex-husband and children. She claimed they were living together better after their divorce than they had while they were married in the conventional sense. They seemed to have love, companionship and support—plus the opportunity to date other people.

My Marriage Experience

So how did I approach marriage? I confess that when I asked Michele to marry me, I was *afraid*. I knew I was attracted to her, and I wanted to settle down. But the thought of making such a binding decision was daunting.

I hate to admit that I proposed to Michele on the telephone. We were living over 200 miles apart. After hesitantly popping the question, I felt a momentary surge of excitement when she said yes. Then after she hung up, I got nervous again. I thought, *Oh, boy, what have I done? Is this the right thing? Am I up to the challenge?* Of course, there are two sides to every story, so I've asked Michele to share her marriage expectations with you.

The euphoria of courtship, the Hollywood mythology of romance and my own self-induced deception painted a picture of the man I would marry: suave, debonair, tall, dark, mysterious, sensitive, macho, with deep pockets like a Rockefeller.

While sitting in dimly lit restaurants listening to the dreams of this handsome visionary, I began to envision what life would be like as Mrs. Harry R. Jackson, Jr. My first mistake was to stop listening to him and begin filling in the blanks, spinning a yarn in my subconscious. I created a fantasy of what our lives together would be like.

On the dance floor, the nostalgia of all the old love stories filled my head as he held me close, whispering in my ear. Entertaining childhood and teenage-girl fantasies, while nursing the desire to be rescued, I developed an image of a man who could walk on water while chewing on paper and spitting out money. He was to be the answer to all of my problems. Yet in the pit of my stomach I knew I had too many problems for any one person to solve.

Nevertheless, the euphoria that accompanied the dream of being rescued created such a sense of well-being that it was hard to face reality. He was Prince Charming, my knight in shining armor.

Then reality set in! As our starry-eyed state of newlywed bliss began to wear off, we started encountering problems. Misunderstandings grew more frequent. Annoying habits appeared. Disagreements about roles surfaced. Differences started cropping up that we hadn't noticed before. It wasn't long before it dawned on us: "Wow, this marriage stuff is a lot of work!"

It's situations like this that bring couples to a fork in the road. They can choose the road *less* traveled—confronting their problems and working through them in a healthy, constructive way. Or they can choose the road *more* traveled—avoiding conflict and dodging potentially painful issues. Of course, the more severe the problems, the harder it is to confront them. Many couples spend years vacillating—not really happy, but afraid to upset the status quo.

Other Marriage Experiences

When I address this subject with audiences or in counseling sessions, I often mention the Shakespearean play *Hamlet* to illustrate the repercussions of indecision. Hamlet's famous soliloquy reminds us of the most troubling aspects of the average marriage. "Slings and arrows" may sound like some verbal exchanges you have had with your spouse. "Sea of troubles" may describe your financial situation or relational history.

Hamlet's family was in desperate need of help. Hamlet's uncle secretly murdered his brother (Hamlet's father) and then stole the crown to rule the kingdom. This uncle then married Hamlet's mother. When the ghost of Hamlet's father demanded revenge, the young man prepared to kill his uncle. But discovering the man kneeling in prayer, Hamlet couldn't bear to murder him. Hamlet felt like a coward because he couldn't avenge his father's slaying. Later he contemplated suicide because the pressure was so great. (Do you think this sounds unbelievably complicated? If so, you haven't been involved in church counseling sessions!)

The entire Shakespearean drama boils down to a single question that Hamlet asks of himself.

> To be or not to be, that is the question: Whether 'tis nobler in the mind to suffer the slings and arrows of outrageous fortune, or to take arms against a sea of troubles. And by opposing end them? To die: to sleep; no

more; and by sleep say we end the heartache and the thousand natural shocks that this flesh is heir to, 'tis a consummation devoutly to be wished.[2]

Hamlet wondered if he should act on what he knew or commit suicide to avoid the pain that life had brought him. He did not act decisively, and his ambivalence had tragic results. By the end of the play, the love of his life was dead, along with her father and both of Hamlet's parents.

Indecision is sometimes a decision in itself. Refusal to face marital problems only allows them to worsen. If we do not aggressively address our problems in light of the Word of God, we invite emotional, spiritual or relational death by default.

Many couples are at a place where they know decisive measures must be taken. But change takes effort, courage and time. Some people commit emotional suicide in order to cope with life. They'd rather die than change. Some of the mechanisms used to commit this type of suicide are addictions (food, sex, drugs, alcohol), which are often used to numb pain and to avoid facing reality and their problems.

> **Indecision is sometimes a decision in itself. Refusal to face marital problems only allows them to worsen.**

TOUGH CHOICES

Let me tell you about one of the most difficult choices Michele and I had to make. In the winter of 1985, we had just celebrated eight years of marriage. We were living in a lovely new home, designed like a ski chalet, on two acres of land overlooking the charming town of Corning, New York. Deer would often appear in our backyard. In fall, wild turkeys waddled down our front driveway. Our dream house was in a dream location—perfect for raising children.

I was working full-time as a national sales and marketing manager for a Fortune 500 company. I had just been promoted to a post that gave me responsibility for $14 million worth of business. Some folks thought I was on a fast track to becoming a corporate vice president.

But there was a problem—I was also pastoring a three-year-old church that had grown from six people to nearly 100. I traveled two or three days a week with my job and spent most of my free time at church activities and with parishioners. Although Michele didn't work outside the home then, she handled all the day-to-day management of our fledgling ministry and cared for our daughter, Joni, who was approaching four years of age. To put it mildly, we were maxed out! There was virtually no time to nurture our marriage, and Joni was often given the leftover hours and energy.

I'll never forget the night Michele declared that I had to make a decision.

"This is crazy!" she said with enough forcefulness to get my attention. "We're exhausted, overwhelmed and stressed out. We can't go on like this. I don't care about the money. Something's got to change!"

The fact is, I totally agreed with her. So we sat down together and talked about the kind of lifestyle that would please God and us. Together we made three decisions that changed our marriage.

1. We would pastor the church together.
2. I would resign from my corporate management position.
3. I would prioritize time with Michele and Joni.

On paper, these seemed like reasonable, rational decisions. In reality, they were extremely hard to make. As a result of my decision to work in full-time ministry, I took a 70 percent pay cut, and we were forced to sell our beautiful home.

I'll be honest, it often pained me as I considered the loss of that house and income. But I know we did the right thing. I never regretted the opportunity to spend more time with Michele and Joni (and later, our other daughter, Liz). The last three years we spent in Corning were very memorable. I was actually present—in body, mind and spirit—for major events in my daughters' lives. Prior to the career change, I would often show up physically while my mind was distracted and my spirit dragging. Whatever success we have achieved in our family is the result of focusing on the quality of life we had together. I thank God for the wisdom He deposited in Michele to help me come to a point of change.

MARRIAGE SETBACKS

I've counseled many couples who made an earnest decision to pursue greatness in their marriage in order to honor God. But some of these people could never seem to turn their convictions into reality. Something was thwarting their progress. As I've studied this issue, I've come to the realization that three common problems keep marriages stuck even when couples ardently desire change. Let's look at each in turn.

A Serious Heart Condition

I'm not talking about a physical heart problem. The Bible uses the word "heart" to describe the intersection of emotional, psychological and spiritual aspects of our lives. Proverbs 4:23 tells us, "Above all else, guard your heart, for it is the wellspring of life." Life flows out of the heart. If there are problems within that have not been dealt with, we will find it difficult to develop the great marriage we desire.

Some years ago, our church owned a facility that had an interesting water problem in one of the offices. The water would come out red when the tap was first turned on. After the water ran for 10 or 15 minutes it would become clear. The impurity existed whether we saw the reddish color or not. Replacing the 50-year-old plumbing would have been the only cure, but this was too expensive. We kept putting it off, and we eventually sold the building having never solved the problem.

This is a picture of what happens in our lives when we have impurities in our hearts that build up over time. Hebrews 12:15 says that a root of bitterness springs up and defiles many. But bitterness is only one heart problem. Some people have fear of abandonment or an irrational need to be the center of attention. Even a lack of love can taint or pervert the quality of our lives. A myriad of mind-sets and attitudes exist that choke out the love-producing power of the Word.

For many years, I struggled with the heart condition of workaholism and "the success trap." I was driven by my need for significance, and I tried to achieve that by doing more, working harder and earning people's accolades. This trap led me to believe I was worthwhile only when I measured up to everyone's expectations—performed flawlessly—and said yes to every request that came to me.

It's easy to see how this heart condition damaged my family life. I was so busy trying to win approval and acceptance in my work and ministry that my wife and children were shortchanged. For years I had "working vacations" or caught some needed sleep on holidays only because the church office was not open. Ultimately a vicious cycle evolved. When Michele would confront me about my out-of-balance lifestyle, I'd feel cornered. So I would escape to work where I felt competent and appreciated. The more she spoke about her need for time together, the wider the chasm grew between us.

Thankfully, God began to perform heart surgery on me. I started to feel exhausted and worn down. Michele's words began to make sense. I realized that Joni and Liz had suffered much because I was always busy with someone else's problems. I seemed to be more patient with parishioners than with my own family. And the numerous family incidents served as a true wake-up call for me.

For instance, several years ago I was counseling a family I'll call the Johnsons. The parents were experiencing major problems and seemed headed toward divorce. The husband had been involved with other women, the wife constantly badgered and belittled him, and they bickered constantly. They were in trouble! When my wife mentioned the Johnsons in relation to some church function, 13-year-old Joni blurted out, "Oh, the Johnsons? They're great. They are a really close-knit family—not like us. They're really connected."

I was shocked. I thought, *Did she just say the Johnsons are really close-knit—"not like us"? Is that how she really views our family?* Although I didn't respond, Joni's words cut me like a knife and they began to haunt me. I knew I needed to make some changes, so I made a conscious effort to spend more time at home. I also began looking for ways to spend extended time with my daughters.

One opportunity came during a Thanksgiving break when Joni was a college freshman and Elizabeth a high school freshman. My wife had a speaking engagement in England, and I found a great deal on airline tickets for my daughters. I successfully turned my wife's business trip into a "Jackson Family Adventure in England." My daughters and I toured and shopped for three days while Mom worked, and all of us spent wonderful times together in the evenings. It was a trip our family will never forget! Who knows if I would've done such a thing in my earlier workaholic years?

Finally God also spoke to me through His Word as I meditated on particular passages.

Am I now trying to win the approval of men, or of God? Or am I trying to please men? If I were still trying to please men, I would not be a servant of Christ (Gal. 1:10).

We speak as men approved by God to be entrusted with the gospel. We are not trying to please men but God, who tests our hearts (1 Thess. 2:4).

If anyone does not provide for his relatives, and especially for his immediate family, he has denied the faith and is worse than an unbeliever (1 Tim. 5:8). (I took this to mean providing for them emotionally as well as financially.)

It's important to remember that few of us are without some heart condition that hinders family growth. Is there a deep-seated issue you need to address? I urge you to do so, because your decision to seek help will begin to bring wholeness to yourself and your family.

A Lack of Closure to Past Problems

Although marriage is presented as a new start for the bride and groom, they still take their old selves into the union. Unhealthy patterns, childhood traumas, unaddressed emotional wounds, ineffective ways of relating or any number of issues can be carried into the marriage relationship. Sadly, some couples believe problems will vanish when they say, "I do." Psychologist Neil Clark Warren reports on this subject.

Many people think marriage will be a magical cure for their problems, that their old struggles will disappear as soon as they tie the knot. And perhaps for a while the freshness and exhilaration of their relationship hides signs of trouble. The newlyweds think, *It's a new beginning. We're going to leave the old problems behind and start over.*

But inevitably, marriage only intensifies problems. The stress of marriage, the vulnerability of living with someone day in and day out, the weight of responsibility, the fear of failure, the realization that marriage isn't a cure-all—all of these combine to thrust existing problems to the forefront.[3]

Sometimes the baggage carried into marriage involves character issues—lying, cheating, gossiping, jealousy and so on. We need to work on these deficiencies—hopefully prior to getting married—or they'll be like 100-pound weights dragging down our relationship.

At other times, premarital traumas exist in our lives that require counseling. These might include emotional or physical abuse, sexual issues, our parents' divorce, serious illness or the death of a loved one. Some years ago I met a young woman whose first husband had drowned in a boating accident. It was very difficult for this woman to overcome the fear that bodily harm could come to her family. So she became a control freak in an attempt to keep danger away. Her sons were placed under heavy restrictions, and she viewed her new husband's fun-loving approach to life as being irresponsible and reckless. This wonderful woman viewed her entire life through the colored lenses of a past trauma. She needed extensive counseling before her marriage and family could be happy.

Secret sins—infidelity, pornography use, hidden drinking and so on—also greatly hinder marital communication and connection. Just as Adam and Eve's personal sins separated them from God and each other, we as married persons in the 21st century can experience the same problems. The fig leaves that Adam and Eve wore did not shield them from the eyes of God. Their disobedience to God's laws created distance in their relationship as well. The spiritual and emotional condition of being naked and unashamed represents a life in which sin is confessed—not hidden or suppressed (see Gen. 2:25).

A Lack of Personal Identity

For years I have talked to people who say, "I don't know who I am." So many men and women have not come to understand who they are, why they're on Earth and how they're supposed to live their lives. They have yet to discover the unique person God created them to be.

It's almost impossible to help someone else (your spouse and kids) feel good about themselves if you don't feel good about yourself. The Lord has ordained that each person have a sense of personal dignity and value. God said in Genesis 1:26, "'Let us make man in our image, in our likeness.'" He thought highly enough of each of us to place His image within us. We have creative ability and emotional sensitivity crafted by God Himself.

Many people lack a healthy self-image because their identity is not based on God's Word. Basic Christian disciplines will assist you and your spouse in developing a healthy identity— Bible reading, Scripture memorization, prayer and meditation on meaningful passages. I recommend you study and meditate on all the passages that tell you who you are in Christ.

It is because of him that you are in Christ Jesus, who has become for us wisdom from God—that is, our righteousness, holiness and redemption (1 Cor. 1:30).

Now it is God who makes both us and you stand firm in Christ. He anointed us, set his seal of ownership on us, and put his Spirit in our hearts as a deposit, guaranteeing what is to come (2 Cor. 1:21-22).

Therefore, if anyone is in Christ, he is a new creation; the old has gone, the new has come! (2 Cor. 5:17).

In love he predestined us to be adopted as his sons through Jesus Christ (Eph. 1:4-5).

In him we have redemption through his blood, the forgiveness of sins, in accordance with the riches of God's grace that he lavished on us (Eph. 1:7-8).

The grace of our Lord was poured out on me abundantly, along with the faith and love that are in Christ Jesus (1 Tim. 1:14).

By building our self-esteem on God's Word, we will gain a biblical framework for our lives. Improving our emotional and spiritual health is sure to benefit our closest relationships.

Additionally, another way to shore up a shaky self-image is to develop meaningful same-sex friendships. God's plan for us is to be in close relationships where "iron sharpens iron" (Prov. 27:17). As we are encouraged, affirmed and cheered on by friends and mentors, we will learn to see ourselves as God sees us. In numerous Scripture passages, we are told to draw strength and encouragement from brothers and sisters in Christ.

Let us consider how we may spur one another on toward love and good deeds. Let us not give up meeting together, as some are in the habit of doing, but let us encourage one another (Heb. 10:24-25).

Many men in our culture (and an increasing number of women) find themselves isolated, cut off from meaningful relationships. Men tend to wait for a crisis to occur before they share emotionally with others. But God designed us to benefit from the accountability, insights and encouragement of others—not occasionally but regularly. It's time to put what the Hebrews writer said into practice.

THE GROWTH PROCESS

Our growth as individuals, couples and families is a continual process. Each stage of life brings unique challenges and opportunities; therefore, we must regularly choose to nurture and improve our marriages. The way to ensure ongoing growth is to practice personal and family lordship of Christ. This means that every aspect of our lives is progressively surrendered to Christ. As soon as we see something out of alignment, we need to bring that area into compliance with the demands of Christ and His Word. Christ's lordship in our families implies that committed parents move their families as a unit into obedience to the Word of God.

I describe the growth process of a family by using the analogy of building codes. If you are building a new home, all architectural plans have to include new changes in codes. However, many existing houses are exempt from having to comply with the updated regulations. These exemptions are called grandfather clauses. These homes are exempt from complying with the current codes because they were already approved under less rigid standards.

While grandfather exemptions work well in the building industry, we operate by different standards in God's kingdom. Ephesians 2:22 says that "you too are being built together to become a dwelling in which God lives by his Spirit." Here our household is spoken of as a living building that is (1) constructed and (2) keeps on growing. This implies that we cannot use grandfather clauses as our excuse for lack of growth. Our spiritual buildings must conform to new and higher standards as we continue to grow in Christ.

The building inspector in our situation is the Holy Spirit. He informs us of changes in code through sermons we hear, conferences we attend or passages of Scripture made real to us through personal devotions. Family calamities or external circumstances dramatically demonstrate our need to grow. The birth of a sickly child, the learning problems of our teenager or the need to care for an elderly relative can suddenly reveal new "building codes" for our marriages and families.

So how can we monitor growth? We must rate our marriages by asking questions related to God's mission for families, which I referred to at the beginning of this chapter.

- Are we more fulfilled than we were two years ago? Despite the headaches and hassles encountered by our family, is there a foundation of joy in our lives? Remember, fulfillment is not based on happiness that results from events. Instead, it is a sense of destiny and hopefulness about the future.
- Is our home a light for God's kingdom? How many specific individuals have become interested in Christ as they have interacted with our family? How many of our family, friends or acquaintances want to model themselves after our marriage? How many of our peers ask us how we handle difficulties?

We are in a struggle to achieve all of the good described in God's Word for our lives. We want to hear the Lord say at the end of our lives, "Well done, good and faithful servant!" not "Well thought" or "Well intentioned." "Well done" implies that we set a goal and went for it. We ran with perseverance the race marked out before us to gain victory (see Heb. 12:1). We made a choice and followed through on it. We determined to make Jesus Christ the Lord of our marriage and family, and we've taken steps to achieve that goal.

To be or not to be the kind of awesome family God wants you to be? Now *that* is the question!

LET PEACE PREVAIL

Four Elements of Family Harmony

All love that has not friendship for its base is like a mansion built upon the sand.

Ella Wheeler Wilcox, "Upon the Sand"

When I mention the name General George Armstrong Custer, what immediately springs to mind? A cavalry leader who led his troops straight into the Little Big Horn massacre, right?

In fact, General Custer enjoyed an illustrious military career. His training, experience and skills had ensured several battlefield successes. He even looked the part of a valiant soldier with his rugged, robust visage. If not for that tragic final defeat, he might have gone down in history as a real American hero. Instead, his legacy has been tarnished. Folklore, Hollywood and popular literature present him as an icon of presumption and pride.

Some married people are like Custer in this sense. They have all the tools for success—training, skills and abilities—but they lead themselves and others toward an unexpected disaster (unless big changes are made). I've met many people who have regretted their relational mistakes for years and probably will for the rest of their lives.

In contrast to General Custer's real-life band of soldiers, *McHale's Navy* represented a fictional group of zany men who were thrown into World War II by necessity. *McHale's Navy* was a popular '60s TV show and was made into a movie in 1997. Who were the men in this navy? They were overweight, poorly dressed military rejects. Fate alone had connected them with each other. Originally, the only goal for this bungling group was to get out of the war alive. But as they strove together for this goal, they learned the arts of unconditional love, listening to each other and laughing at their own mistakes.

Is your family more like Custer's army, marching toward ruin, or McHale's navy, learning to work together for victory? Is your family, even with a lot of skills and smarts, heading for disaster? Or are you, even with quirks and foibles, pulling together to ensure success?

I'm happy to say that McHale's navy more closely describes my household. Consider Michele's perspective of our family life.

Home can be a haven or a hornet's nest. Early in our marriage, I decided that my home would be a haven—a place where the peace, presence, provision and power of Jesus would be seen in practical ways.

When our children were small, I was able to control *everything* in their lives. Outside influences, visitors, reading materials and food items consumed were all under the scrutiny of "the warden." Once they started school and began attending activities where Jesus was not the primary focus, I had to keep the lines of communication open.

It was not long before their choices became tough: Jesus or friends? Jesus or activities? Things have a way of subtly piling up and producing a logjam. No matter how hard you try to keep it under control, things can change quickly.

So we began to have family conferences, where we discussed issues like convenience versus commitment, witnessing versus evangelizing, maintaining integrity versus succumbing to peer pressure. Tempers, tears and tantrums were usually a part of the family conferences, but that was all right—at least we were still talking.

I often reminded my daughters that the primary goal of their lives was to be women of God. We discussed what it meant to put Jesus first in our lives. We consciously prioritized our activities by asking, "Would a woman of God be involved in that activity? Would Jesus attend this party with me?" These conferences really helped us stay close.

Michele's point about her ability to control the home environment in the early days is significant, because it helped our family as we grew in age and maturity—recognizing that the quality of our relationships was the primary thing that kept our home God-honoring. Keeping legalistic Christian rules has not been the basis of my relationship with my wife, but cultivating a Christ-centered relationship has. This doesn't "just happen" though. It is a process that takes time, attention and maintenance. Like Custer's army versus McHale's navy, the difference lies in the strength of its relationships. We discovered that a family also experiences similar differences.

THE POWER OF PARADIGM

I will never forget the September 11 terrorist attack on Washington, D.C. Our staff offices at that time were downtown, not far from Pennsylvania Avenue, where the White House and many monuments stand. A group of us had gathered for a daily prayer session. When we received the report about New York, our prayer meeting took a decisive turn. Minutes later, we were told of the attack on our city.

As we evacuated our building, we noticed scores of disoriented people piling into cars and lining up to get on the Beltway. Everyone was asking the same questions: "How did the enemy get into our territory? How could they attack us on our own soil?"

These are the same questions many families ask about the turmoil and pain that erupts out of nowhere within their homes.

The rising divorce rate among church leaders seems to be as shocking to some as a terrorist attack. A 2001 *Newsweek* article stated that as many as 30 percent of male Protestant ministers have been sexually active with women other than their wives.[1] What's more, the divorce rate among U.S. pastors has risen 65 percent over the past 25 years.[2] Just as in the case of the hijacked airlines on September 11, protective measures that should have been observed within these clergy members' homes were ignored.

I am not picking on pastors—after all, statistics about divorce and infidelity pertaining to *all* Christians are mighty bleak. My point is that God has ordained a powerful security system for our families, and we must diligently safeguard our relationships. When a family is in biblical balance, the home is a place of safety and peace. Tragedy often occurs when precautions and biblical principles are ignored.

Satan's primary objective in spiritual warfare is to attack relationships and, thereby, separate us from God and others. He's just like other predators who isolate their victims in order to devour them as easy prey. How can we unify and protect ourselves? George S. Patton, deemed by many to be a military genius, gave a simple but profound clue: "All the links in the chain pull together, and the chain becomes unbreakable."[3]

Unfortunately, many families today are pulling apart rather than pulling together. Parents and kids are going separate ways and pursuing their own agendas. They drive to places in their own cars and then retreat to their own bedrooms at home. What's more, family members are busy fighting their own private wars. Kids fight the battles of insecurity, peer pressure and raging hormones. Dad is frustrated with his job, the finances and his retirement plan. Mom is dealing with parenting problems, depression and a never-ending to-do list. Too often, epic personal battles are fought without other family members even knowing about them. We may feel like the golden-haired Custer facing a horde of enemy warriors charging our unsecured position.

> **God has ordained a powerful security system for our families, and we must diligently safeguard our relationships.**

What we need in order to build up our relationships is a biblical framework or paradigm. These paradigms help us to *act on* the biblical command to love and respect our spouse. They enable us to *carry out* the admonition to nurture and encourage our family members. The apostle Paul tells us:

> There should be no division in the body, but that its parts [members] should have equal concern for each other. If one part suffers, every part suffers with it; if one part is honored, every part rejoices with it (1 Cor. 12:25-26).

This is God's plan for the Church, and it is undoubtedly His plan for individual families as well.

T.R.U.E. LOVE

To have harmony in our families, we need what I call T.R.U.E. relationships. This acrostic—Trust, Respect, Understanding and Expressed Love—designates four relational aspects vital to developing strength and vigor. Incorporating these components into our relationships will be like erecting four reinforced walls around a fortress. Any family that desires strength in Christ and secure love for each other must build these elements into their relationship.

Trust

The writer of Proverbs asks: "Many a man claims to have unfailing love, but a faithful man who can find?" (20:6). In the context of a family, faithfulness and the trust it produces are not *found*— they are *created*. Trust is not something that automatically occurs because two people take marriage vows. If two young people think that they'll make it through all of life's challenges simply because they are *so in love*, I've got some news for them: Hearts are knit together and stay together because couples make a commitment to build upon the foundation of trust.

The world is filled with ideas and mind-sets that work against long-term relationships and the biblical concept of family. Many women cynically say, "Men don't think with their heads—their libidos think for them! You just can't trust a man. He'll always try to trade you in for a younger model." Conversely, men in our generation often fear that their wives are trying to control them or marriage seems like a scheme for wives to pigeonhole or henpeck their husbands.

However, having a healthy, trusting marriage doesn't mean we will not have conflict. Sometimes we get worried when disagreements crop up. But if we address these problems, short-term conflict may lead to more peace in the future. It is often the unaddressed issues that increase emotional distance and mistrust. After years of relational drift, you could wake up one morning feeling married to an intimate stranger.

As I have counseled couples over the years, I have repeatedly seen that adultery destroys trust. After infidelity, the next greatest destroyer of trust in a marriage is lying. Many women lie about their spending habits and purchases in attempts to avoid conflict. Men often embellish the truth to avoid looking incompetent. These little white lies seem so easy and convenient that their impact seems inconsequential; however, this is usually not the case.

Respect

Is your spouse rude to you? Does he or she fail to think about you when making decisions? Does your husband ignore you when you ask a question? Does your wife subtly belittle you in front of the children? Is there an absence of manners or common courtesy? If so, these may be signs revealing a lack of respect in your marriage.

If you feel disrespected and you don't spell these issues out to your mate, he or she may never "get it." We must be clear in these areas if we want changes to occur. Women may not understand why they continue to feel unworthy in a relationship or why they keep giving to a family that doesn't show appreciation. This wife or mother may be compensating for a lack of respect. She may be trying to earn the respect she ought to be getting for free. Women in our culture are often wired to respond to the approval—or lack of approval—of their husbands and kids.

Many times, husbands feel more like packhorses than people. They are carrying emotional and financial burdens for the family without the honor they felt their fathers received. Michael Baisden, author of *Never Satisfied: How and Why Men Cheat*, asserts that lack of respect is one of the major reasons men cheat on their wives.[4] Feeling admired and accepted by another woman can be too tempting for a man to resist if he is not receiving respect at home.

Sometimes a man may feel as though his wife's complaints about his behavior is not just nagging, but a lack of respect for who he is. Then why does he make this mental leap from repeated discussions about cleaning the house or too much time at the gym to feeling disrespected? It may not be much of a leap after all. Take a look at the following example.

The wife may respond, "But that's how *my* mom and dad related!" If your husband is feeling devalued, you will need a different approach to your next conversation. Many women confronted with recurring problems repeat the same statements, only more loudly or more frequently. They don't realize that they are literally driving their husbands into defiant resistance— and perhaps into the arms of another woman.

For men, it is becoming increasingly difficult to make a living, give clear guidance to the family and be an adequate spouse. Most men are wired to want to play the role of a hero. Unfortunately, the nature of the daily grind does not leave many Harrison Ford or Tom Cruise personas. For this reason, a wife's affirmation and the respect of his children become even more important to a man facing the challenges of this generation.

The erosion of respect also manifests itself in the deterioration of common courtesy and good manners. After you have lived with someone for many years, there is a tendency for life's big problems and little annoyances to wear you down. You can begin to think less of the gifted individual with whom you live.

When it comes to demonstrating courtesy, husbands often fall short. They fail to open doors for their wives, lift heavy packages, help clean the kitchen or give compliments. Courtesies such as these say, "You are valued and appreciated." It's not uncommon for a man to fuss more over the comfort of a visitor than the comfort of his spouse. Wives can also be callous to the needs of their husbands for affirmation, appreciation, words of encouragement and sexual attentiveness.

Understanding

There's no doubt that men and women are wired differently. Their needs, temperaments, communication styles and approaches to problem solving are often poles apart. John Gray, author of *Men Are from Mars, Women Are from Venus*, emphasizes how these differences may lead to misunderstandings.

> No matter how committed we are to improving our relationships, it is impossible to make significant advances without reevaluating our hidden assumptions. . . . We assume that we are the same when, in many ways, men and women are as different as aliens from separate planets would be.[5]

In family counseling sessions, I often hear wives or children blurt out, "Nobody listens to me! I've been trying to tell them how I feel for months." The impatient wife will weep because she feels unheard. She believes she is misunderstood and her family is minimizing and discounting her pain.

When a relationship is in trouble, it can resemble two people standing in the tunnel of Horseshoe Falls in Niagara, Canada. They are in the most romantic place in the world, yet they are shouting over the roar of the water to be heard. It's as if the hurting spouses are screaming out their own needs so loudly that they cannot hear or emotionally process the needs of the other person.

However, at times you might feel that you've done everything to get your point across, but your partner still doesn't seem to hear. Sometimes when I am with a troubled couple, I'll ask them to write down the three most pressing needs of their relationship. The order is significant because it reveals each spouse's sense of pressure and/or urgency. When I compare what the husband and wife have written, they hardly ever have the same issues listed in the same order. Breakthroughs often begin when spouses come to understand *why* certain needs are so important to each other.

The misunderstood spouse may want to think about three aspects of communication. I'll call these the *bridge-building triad*. First, learn the language of your spouse's hobby or special interest. For example, a wife might describe her frustration with the finances in football or golf terms. A husband may use cooking or gardening analogies to help bridge the communication gap.

Second, pick your time and place to communicate carefully. Spouses often don't communicate effectively because they aren't in the frame of mind to genuinely hear each other. For example, if you are a morning person and your spouse is a night owl, don't expect to have a meaningful discussion at 6:00 A.M. Instead, meet halfway. Have important discussions over lunch or in the early evening. Similarly, don't try to talk while the television is on or when your three-year-old is sitting on your lap. Find a place that's conducive to conversation.

Third, practice describing your situation with someone who knows you well (unless, of course, the information is sensitive and private). Often we *think* we're expressing ourselves clearly, but something gets lost in the translation. A neutral third party can often tell if you are communicating plainly and precisely.

Of course, it's not only spouses who sometimes feel misunderstood. Children often feel the same way. If this is the case in your household, spend a lot of time listening to your children talk about struggles. Don't judge or criticize what your child says, and don't rush to offer solutions. Just listen with an open mind and heart. At the end of any account ask questions such as, "And how did that make you feel?" (We'll discuss communication at length in chapter 5.)

Expressed Love

How do we demonstrate love to our close family members? How do they know we are maintaining our concern, love and respect for them? We need to make sure we're showing love in a way that clearly communicates our intent. Our acts must speak love in a language that's understood by the recipient.

Author Gary Chapman has made a major contribution to my life and the members of my church through his teaching about the five love languages.[6] Chapman believes that spoken words are not the only important way to convey caring. He has identified five languages by which people express and understand love: quality time, gift-giving, words of affirmation, acts of service and physical touch. We must identify which of these is most valuable to our family members and then use that language to communicate on their wavelengths.

No matter what your primary love language is, verbal communication is still important in every relationship. Many wives and mothers are better at communicating love than their male counterparts. Many men have never heard their fathers say "I love you" in a caring and consistent way. These words are often mumbled to sons in an under-the-breath, eyes-adverted or emotionally clumsy manner.

It's hard to move from being an in-control office worker or tough jock to a compassionate husband and father who voices his feelings of love. Not many of us can imagine Clint Eastwood or Sylvester Stallone having a sentimental, heart-to-heart conversation with his family. Men often feel as though their love is expressed through heroic actions. However, this expression of love is not easily expressed with words, which is what a lot of women appreciate. Nevertheless, in order to grow into maturity as followers of Christ, each person has to cultivate and learn to express emotional love.

THE INGREDIENTS OF TRUST

Of the four elements in the T.R.U.E. relationship paradigm, trust is the most complex. For if I don't feel that I am respected, understood or loved, I will not trust. This is also the element that if present provides a safe environment so other issues can be addressed. Once trust is established, my wife and I can work through financial challenges, sexuality expectations, parenting problems and so on.

But what if trust has been violated in your family, either by you or by someone else? I believe there are six steps to rebuilding trust. To explain these, I'll use the metaphor of baking a cake. Each step in the baking process parallels the relationship-building process, and someone must take responsibility for creating this environment of relational growth. This person is like a chef who mixes all the ingredients together. Tie on your apron and let's examine the six steps.

Clear the Countertop

To do the job right, a cook needs to clean up old messes and begin with a tidy countertop and washed utensils. If baking pans, spoons and spatulas are not properly cleaned, residual bacteria may be present. These can defile and contaminate the batter of the cake. So all the crud and dirt must be washed away before the cook can proceed.

In relationships, we too need a fresh start. As Proverbs 17:9 tells us, "He who covers over [or forgives] an offense promotes love." This means working through past hurts and forgiving the person in whom we've lost confidence. Forgiveness allows the healing to begin—but that doesn't mean it's easy. Depending upon the severity of the offense, it may take months or even years to forgive one another.

The writer of Hebrews says:

Make every effort to live in peace with all men and to be holy; without holiness no one will see the Lord. See to it that no one misses the grace of God and that no bitter root grows up to cause trouble and defile many (12:14-15).

Extracting a bitter root means we have to forgive those who have hurt us and release them from our desire to avenge. If old hurts exist, they must be dealt with thoroughly and completely before the restoration of trust can begin.

Read the Labels

A chef might consider adding yeast to the cake mix to help it rise. However, a quick scan of the label would advise otherwise: Though yeast works well with bread, it would destroy a cake. To make the dessert edible and tasty, she has to follow the recipe exactly. Replacing or changing the amount of one ingredient could alter the cake's taste and appearance.

When it comes to marriage, you have to understand the true nature of your partner. If you start with an insecure wife, you must add a lot of encouragement and reassurance. If your husband has been plagued by guilt and shame all of his life, you need to mix in plenty of grace and acceptance. The same principle applies to children. If your son loves to flout rules and challenge authority, you'll need an extra measure of boundary setting and consequences for misbehavior.

What's more, we must be open to differences in the character, opinions and personality traits of our family members. I don't agree with all the advice offered by Dr. Phil McGraw (a regular on the *Oprah* show), but I like this point.

> Sometimes we feel that because something is not main-stream, then it must be toxic to the relationship, and that's not necessarily true. Everyone has quirks and odd personality traits, and they can sometimes seem bizarre. If your partner's quirks and nuances are nonabusive to you and nondestructive to him or her, you can work on them.[7]

Many of our disappointments are the result of misjudging and misinterpreting other people. We may have counted on them for things they could not produce. We want them to be like *us*, but they're not. God made them unique individuals. Accepting them as they are creates an environment where trust can grow and flourish.

Mix in All the Ingredients

A chef knows which ingredients are essential and which are optional. She might substitute chocolate for coconut in order to flavor the cake differently, but if she neglects to put in the basic ingredients—flour, eggs and shortening—the result would be a culinary catastrophe.

Two essential ingredients for any relationship are grace and affirmation. We see these qualities demonstrated by Jesus over and over again in the Gospels. To the Samaritan woman who had five husbands, He showed compassion and understanding (see John 4:7-42). To the woman caught in adultery He said, "'Neither do I condemn you . . . Go now and leave your life of sin'" (John 8:11). Likewise, the parable Jesus told about the prodigal son features a loving father—symbolic of our heavenly Father—who rejoiced when his wayward son returned home (see Luke 15:11-32).

When someone has offended us and we're beginning to rebuild trust, we are acutely aware of his or her shortcomings. We fear reinjury, so we erect a protective fence by continually reminding the other person what caused the breach in the first place.

Yet this is not the time to preach about change. Instead, we must add grace and affirmation. Reassure them of your love, as Jesus so often did. At this point, all we can do is assemble the right ingredients and trust that God's recipe will not fail.

Stir and Bake

Great chefs know that there is a certain mystery in the baking process that is beyond their control. They may not understand the chemistry involved when all those ingredients coalesce to create something delicious; they just know it works! Once the recipe has been followed and the oven set properly, they have to trust that the cake will bake to perfection.

In the same way, once all the elements are in place in our families, we must trust God to work in His mysterious ways. We must believe the words of the apostle Paul, who said, "He who began a good work in you will carry it on to completion" (Phil. 1:6). Changes in relationships are never instant. We must recognize that growth is a process and healing takes time. Be patient. Old habits die slowly; new habits take time to develop.

Check on the Cake's Progress

The job isn't yet done when the cake goes into the oven. A chef has to monitor the cake's progress and make sure it's baking correctly. She tests the cake with a toothpick or broom straw and then returns it to the oven if it has a gooey center. She may even have to adjust the temperature. All of this takes vigilance and attentiveness.

Likewise, you must be watchful and observant about how things are progressing in your marriage. You can't assume everything will continue without setbacks. In fact, you may need help to finish the process. Don't be afraid to see a counselor at this stage. If your efforts at personal reconciliation with your husband or wife are not moving forward, get help.

Put the Icing on the Cake

Every chef knows that icing enhances a cake. It makes the cake taste sweet and look aesthetically pleasing. Icing is the finishing touch that completes all the previous steps.

In relationships, thankfulness and celebration are the icing. When trust is restored and healing begun, we must give thanks to God for His amazing grace. We can echo Paul's words when he said, "Thanks be to God! He gives us the victory through our Lord Jesus Christ" (1 Cor. 15:57). We should also celebrate with each other, recognizing that a great work has been done in and through us.

A TRUE STORY ABOUT THE T.R.U.E. PARADIGM

I know a pastor who leads a huge church in a large metropolitan area. Because of his temperament and business training, this pastor was for many years very goal oriented and a perfectionist. If you were standing near him and your tie was crooked, he would've straightened it without thinking. He held himself—and others—to relentlessly high standards.

Unwittingly, he intimidated many people around him. They felt pressured, uneasy and scrutinized. Even though he was in a "people business," he conducted his ministry like a demanding CEO running a corporation rather than a loving shepherd leading a flock. Many of his close relationships and long-term friendships began to dissolve.

Even within this pastor's family, the warmth of relationships had waned. Some friends spoke to him about how his habits and attitude were affecting his wife and two children. In time, he realized he had created a mess at home. As he began to think about remedies, he realized he had a major problem with emotional distance and lack of trust.

The turning point came when this man implemented the T.R.U.E. acrostic as a diagnostic tool, and he began to pursue family harmony and healing. He and his wife had some anger revolving around sexual intimacy. She was often not accessible or available when he needed her. This resentment made him less likely to do nice, romantic things for her. Feeling rejected, he would hide himself in his work where he felt competent.

Improvement came when the pastor tried to show respect by actually listening to the issues his wife had repeatedly brought up (he'd thought of it as nagging before then). When he understood what she needed, he made big changes in his schedule and financial priorities. Before long, she began to think that he really did care about her.

As for his children, their disrespect revolved around the lack of one-on-one time they spent with their father. They felt like neglected employees instead of beloved children. The pastor began to schedule time alone with each one of them three or four times a week. These were not always dates or special outings; sometimes it meant simply driving one of them to school or taking them along for an afternoon of errands. During these times, he would ask their opinions about many things, and he would listen carefully to their answers. Often he would compliment them on little things such as their ability to analyze problems or study languages. In the process, my friend discovered that his children were very gifted.

After the respect-building stage, the pastor began to concentrate on mutual understanding. He recognized that his wife and children didn't know what made him tick. He began to tell them about the midlife struggles he was having as he passed his 40th birthday. They responded by talking about their own struggles and challenges. He had no idea that their lives were so complicated. His children began to seek his counsel instead of confiding only in their mom or friends.

During this phase, the pastor started to feel surges of gratitude and thankfulness to God. He realized that the Lord had blessed him with a tremendous family. This deep sense of appreciation increased his love for them, and he began experimenting with ways to express his feelings. He noted to himself what his wife needed most, and he started to demonstrate his devotion to her through service and words. He became more affectionate and affirming toward his children.

At the end of this journey, the pastor's family had achieved a level of intimacy and trust they'd previously thought impossible. What a close-knit bunch! Although his family is now happy and content, he remains vigilant because he knows that all families are in a state of war. The enemy constantly seeks to reclaim lost territory.

So who is this pastor I'm telling you about in great detail? What—you think it's *me*? I can only confess that this man's journey bears a striking resemblance to my own. And I can further report that I *used to be* a lot like that uptight, driven pastor before he saw the light. I am able to say with great authority—and my family would concur—that the ruthlessly perfectionistic pastor definitely is not me today!

A FINAL WORD

What does a successful marriage and family look like? I am not sure we can measure family success in the typical temporal terms. If we were to look at Custer's military faux pas as a picture of a family's attempt at success, we would conclude that appearance and short-term advancement in career and finances don't mean much. Custer didn't get to grow old with his wife and bounce his grandchildren on his knee. He missed making memories that would have been a lifelong legacy for his kids.

> We need to think of our homes as a refuge, a stronghold we can run to in times of trouble.

However, if McHale's navy were our measure of success, we would rejoice in the fact that a group of imperfect people can come together to achieve something great. Our lives would have meaning because of our vision to further a cause bigger than ourselves. Despite flaws and failures, we could enjoy each other and live in harmony.

As spouses and parents, we need to think of our homes as a refuge, a stronghold we can run to in times of trouble. But fortresses take time to build. The process requires ongoing development of trust, respect, understanding and expressed love. But the reward for all this effort is families that enjoy T.R.U.E. love.

CHAPTER 4

DO YOU KNOW WHERE YOU'RE GOING?

*Creating a Vision and Strategy for
Family Destiny*

*Destiny is not a matter of chance; it is a matter
of choice. It is not something to be waited for,
it is a thing to be achieved.*

William Jennings Bryan, "America's Mission" speech, 1899

An old proverb says, "When you don't know where you are
going, any road will get you there." Sadly, this principle seems to

be the credo—the theme song—for many families today. They have no sense of where they're going or what they want to accomplish together. Many have never given thought to how they can collectively work toward worthwhile goals. Others are so busy dealing with short-term crises and stresses that long-term plans seem unreachable and unrealistic.

Another proverb from the Old Testament tells us that "Where there is no vision, the people perish" (29:18, *KJV*). Let me paraphrase that to say, "without vision, families drift."

In chapter 2, we talked about the need to make a choice to pursue greatness in your marriage and family. Here are four questions we must ask ourselves in regards to the choices we must make for our families.

1. How do my family and I influence others, make a difference and leave a legacy in Christ?
2. How do I measure the impact of my choices?
3. How do I keep my family motivated to walk with me in Christ?
4. How do I keep overwhelming emotions and frustrations to a minimum as I fight "the good fight" for my family? (see 2 Tim. 4:7).

The answer to all four questions is the same: We need specific goals for our families. The goals must be part of a God-given vision, which will provide direction and meaning to our everyday tasks. While each family has a unified goal, it is important that each family member has individual pursuits. This will enhance a family's corporate sense of purpose. Additionally, a realistic vision must have an accompanying strategy or game plan. Strategy is to vision what tracks are to a train—it defines how you will arrive at your destination. We can have all the potential in the world to succeed, but we still need an action plan that can be addressed daily or weekly to reach our goals.

Recognize the Vision

I first realized a need for some kind of vision or long-range planning when I got married at age 23. During college, I had more or less majored in partying, women and drugs. Then after graduation, I lacked any type of direction. In less than two years, I had already tried out for a pro football team, studied acting and taken a job in an unfamiliar city and in an industry I knew nothing about. However, one thing I felt sure about was my interest in business.

My wife, Michele, and I had both rededicated our lives to Christ two months prior to our wedding day. We were on fire for God, expecting His guidance. Still, to say the least, I was not settled on what I wanted to do with my life.

Premarriage Days

Michele will now proceed to explain her perspective on where we were in our premarriage days.

It was hard to believe I was going to become Mrs. Harry R. Jackson, Jr. All of the things I had envisioned as we sat for hours over candlelit dinners had the potential of happening. Mr. Wingtips, the consummate businessman, was going to be my man. We would pursue fame and fortune together.

As the wedding day drew near and my sister Lynn and I shopped for last-minute items, a feeling of giddiness began to fill my stomach. I became nervous, hoping I was making the right decision. Questions filled my mind. Was it going to work out? What about all the divorce and abandonment in my family's previous generations? Was Harry really the person he'd presented? Was I going to wake up the next day with Mr. Hyde? Lynn kept asking, "Shelli, are you okay with this?" But I remembered the deep sense of peace I had when I was around Harry, and I answered, "I am so excited and want to be with him."

On our wedding day, as Lynn and I prepared to leave for the church, Harry stopped me to ask what seemed to be an inappropriate question: "What if I am called to preach?" What timing! He brought this up a few hours before we would pledge to be husband and wife for the rest of our lives. Somewhat dismissive, I replied that as Christians we're all called to proclaim the gospel. Then as I walked out the door, I made it a point to reiterate that he was a businessman and he need not worry about being "called."

As you can see, Michele and I began our marriage with a desperate need to discern God's will. We needed His vision. It was obvious to everyone who knew us that we were dreamers, untested by life's challenges. We believed it would be simple to make a difference for Christ in the world, plus achieve a lucrative lifestyle.

Newlywed Days

In 1977, I was accepted into Harvard Business School. We had been married for only six months. Although I was pleased to receive an acceptance letter, I faced a dilemma. I was trying to decipher God's will and decide whether I wanted training for business or ministry. During that same year, I was also accepted at the University of Chicago and offered a scholarship for the master of divinity program. Strangely, I turned down Harvard in favor of ministry training, and then realized that a lack of relocation funds, unemployment for Michele and other little details would make it impossible to move to Chicago. Now I wouldn't be pursuing either of my choices. What was God doing? I felt as though the rug had been pulled out from under me.

As you can imagine, the following year became quite eventful. Looking back, I can now see that God used my business profession as a maturing process for my faith. As an industrial salesperson, I took Jesus into the marketplace with me, praying over every proposal and every deal. I started on commission with a low base salary, but through the lessons God taught me that year, I nearly tripled my salary by year's end. It was then that I began to see my need for more business training, specifically an MBA. Thus, my decision as to whether to train for ministry or business resurfaced.

I decided to reapply to Harvard in 1978, and we used the reapplication as a "fleece" to confirm our calling to Boston. Harvard accepted me a second time—it was a miracle! Michele and I, now married less than two years, packed our belongings in a U-Haul and drove our little car from Cincinnati to Boston. God had answered, so we followed.

But wait! Why did I go to business school if I knew I'd end up in ministry? Shouldn't I have just gone straight into ministry? Did we misread God's leading? I don't think so, because as I look back, I see how God was training and equipping me for bigger things to come. My time in graduate school and the business world taught me valuable lessons and skills that I would later apply in my ministry. What's more, God knew I had some growing up to do. He used many experiences during that time to mature and refine my character. I thank God that He directed our lives through a vision I had for business. And I especially thank him for providing us with the correct strategy to achieve our goals.

START WITH OBEDIENCE

In the following pages, I will offer several ideas to help you create vision for your family. These concepts will be general, underlying principles. Then I will move on to suggest practical ways to turn these visions into reality.

Before we can grab hold of God's will for us as individuals and families, we must first work and serve Him in His general will. This term—general will—simply means that we seek to follow all of God's commands and principles in the Bible. It seems clear from Scripture that God requires proficiency in the basics before He gives us more responsibility or a higher calling. This is the message of Jesus' parable of the talents. The servant who used his talents wisely was told by his master, "You have been faithful with a few things; I will put you in charge of many things. Come and share your master's happiness!" (Matt. 25:23).

As you can see, we must demonstrate our faithfulness to the basics—honesty, integrity, servanthood and so on—so we can graduate to a specific mission or assignment from the Lord. It was the great preacher and writer Oswald Chambers who said, "The tiniest fragment of obedience, and heaven opens up and the profoundest truths of God are yours straight away. God will never reveal more truth about Himself till you obey what you know already."[1]

Christians are not supposed to set direction for their lives based upon whims or selfish desires alone. Over time, the Lord galvanizes a sense of singular purpose in our hearts, and that purpose is our vision. Our goal should be similar to the apostle Paul's testimony to King Agrippa, "I was not disobedient to the vision from heaven" (Acts 26:19). Paul meant that he obeyed the direct personal assignment of Christ for his life, and it was a vision Paul received from Christ because of his obedience to the basics.

In summary, if I create my own vision, I'll maneuver in my own strength and bring my own plan to pass. But if I have a vision from God, the burden is on Him to direct and assist me. In the same way, God has a personal, specific vision for our families. As we flow in His will, He gives us the help we need.

Know Where You Want to End Up

In Stephen Covey's best-selling book *The Seven Habits of Highly Effective People,* he tells us to "start with the end in mind."[2] In other words, it is very important to know where you want to finish before you start. Covey goes on to describe a picture of putting a ladder against a wall. The ladder represents the method or strategy we choose to accomplish our goals, and the wall represents our destination, the vision we want to fulfill. After experiencing failures or disappointments in life, we may feel a need to refine our vision or replace it altogether. But often we merely change ladders (strategic approaches to our destination). However, changing ladders doesn't help you if you still place a new one against the wrong wall (our ultimate vision or destination).[3]

For instance, suppose I'm living on the beautiful 87-acre site our church owns, and I decide to make some improvements on the property with only $500 to spend. I find an old ladder and prop it against the red barn near the main house and climb to the top. As I start preparing the surface for paint, the wooden ladder starts to break under the stress of my weight. I scramble down and then think to myself, *I need a new ladder and, by the way, I need some paint.* The price of paint for the barn and a new aluminum ladder at a hardware store is only $495! I actually have $5 left over.

I continue to complete the beautification task, exhausting my limited budget. While I sit back and admire my work, I learn two pieces of new information. First, the all-important front fence—which keeps our cattle off the streets—needs to be fixed. Ironically, it could have been done for $500. Second, the barn is going to be torn down in two months to make way for the new sanctuary. Thus, my efforts were futile.

The moral of the story is simple. When the ladder first broke, I should have reevaluated my priorities. Instead, I became more efficient at moving in the wrong direction. I redoubled my efforts—spending more money, time and energy—on the incorrect project. If you are experiencing a sense of futility, disappointment and continual frustration, first consider if you've been heading in the wrong direction. Maybe God is giving you a new vision that will direct you to the right destination.

ASK FOR DIRECTIONS

Moses said of the Israelites, "The LORD went before them by day in a pillar of cloud to lead the way, and by night in a pillar of fire to give them light" (Exod. 13:21, *NKJV*). In the same way, God wants to give us "a pillar of fire"—that clear sense of guidance and direction—if only we'll ask Him.

When our daughter Joni was a sophomore in college, she wanted to help celebrate my birthday. But the trip from Willliams College in Massachusetts to our home in Maryland was too long for her to make. So the day before my birthday, she sent me an e-greetings card. The following morning, she called me on the phone to wish me a happy birthday. And then in the afternoon, I received a Federal Express package, which contained a beautiful gold-colored tie. What a delightful gift!

As I looked in my closet to see what suit this tie would nicely compliment, I noticed about eight other gold ties. I chuckled to myself. Joni had probably spent two hours driving from the campus to the department store to pick out this tie. What she didn't know was that I needed a different-colored tie. I was deeply appreciative of Joni's thoughtfulness but, unfortunately, I didn't get the benefit of all her hard work. I wished she had checked with me before buying the gift.

This story simply reveals that when determining a vision for your family—which is a gift from God—remember to ask the Lord before a final decision is reached or even considered. He does not want you to waste any of your time or effort. Instead, He wants you to give Him something He can use for His kingdom purposes.

BE OPEN TO REDIRECTION

In business, the most successful companies are those that remain flexible and adaptable. They discern market forces and economic shifts and change strategies accordingly. This principle holds true for families as well. Your family's vision may remain the same over a lifetime, or it may need to be updated several times. Often the Lord uses transitions—even painful ones—to redirect us. If we remain malleable, He may bring our lifelong purpose into focus at any point on our journey.

Consider one of the great redirections in the annals of Christendom. Saul—later renamed Paul—was a powerful, well-respected religious leader. His background gave him every advantage for success. He had the family credentials, the right citizenship, the proper education and thorough biblical training. Although all of these were to his benefit, Paul followed the wrong vision. However, during his futile efforts, he had a lightning-bolt experience, an encounter with Christ on the road to Damascus. Jesus explained to Saul that he was persecuting the true Church. His epiphany on that journey rerouted the entire direction of his life. The born-again Paul then pursued his true calling, listening to Christ's new vision and using his established background to glorify God.

In like manner, God never wastes anything in our lives, especially our background. Sometimes the Lord waits to redirect us into His will until we enter a teachable season of life. This is a time in which the Lord knows we'll be open to receive new marching orders—a new vision.

During our lifetime, we shouldn't be so dead-set on pursuing one vision that we're closed to other possibilities. Like Paul, there may be a new wall (direction, destination) for your ladder (strategy). And even if you are seasoned or mature in your faith, your understanding of your personal and family vision may need to be adjusted in order to redirect you from survival to success or from mediocrity to merit. Paul, once the persecutor of Christ, became known as the orator for Christ. Paul ended his life with the testimony that he had finished his race well (see 2 Tim. 4:7). We too can finish our lives with the confidence that we have heeded God's calling and been sensitive to His redirection.

> Sometimes the Lord waits to redirect us into His will until we enter a teachable season of life.

JOIN FORCES

Usually the best visions are those that involve every member of the family. A family vision must encompass everyone's strengths, talents and needs. One member's destiny should not stifle everyone else's opportunities, and there has to be agreement on the personal vision of each member.

What's more, parents need to direct their children's opportunities so they discover their own visions. For example, my kids were given selected choices in the development of their gifts in the early years. When they were younger, we simply said things like, "Choose the instrument you are going to learn, but we want you to take music lessons." And the older they got, the less authoritative we became. While we are a unit with a collective destiny, we are also responsible for helping one another find his or her unique place in God's army. There are three critical factors to the fulfillment of a family vision.

Be a Team Player

Although every team member will have unique talents to offer, the most important goal is team victory, not individual stardom. When I think about teamwork, I consider the team efforts that have had great payoffs: the Joffrey Ballet Company, Michael Jordan and the Chicago Bulls and the Promise Keepers' rally in Washington, D.C. In each of these examples, an overall game plan was executed by gifted people deferring to one another. A team effort can make all the difference, even when it may appear to be a one-man show.

> A family vision must encompass everyone's strengths, talents and needs.

Remember the stories of the infamous sleuth Sherlock Holmes? He certainly had a gift for detective work, but his side-kick, Watson, was no slouch. Watson was a consummate doctor who had Holmes beat on many levels. Yet Sherlock would say to this highly educated physician, "Elementary, my dear Watson," while Watson would have a wonderful way of deferring to his partner, "Oh, Holmes, that's brilliant." Watson expressed an appreciation for Holmes's gift of investigating and solving mysteries. But whenever the story included someone who needed care, it was Watson's turn to shine. They were a perfect team, with clear differentiation of roles and value and respect for each other. Like soldiers in war, they knew they could count on each other.

Within our families, we need this same sense of cooperation and collaboration. We must use our gifts to *complete* one another—not to *compete* with one another.

Promote the Strengths of Others

Even as family members work as a team, each person should feel free to grow and excel individually. Moms and dads, brothers and sisters can identify the strengths in one another and create an environment for growth. It was the legendary football coach Vince Lombardi who said, "A team that has become a winner has done so by individuals setting and reaching goals for themselves."[4] In a healthy family, the success of one member becomes the success of all members.

The apostle Paul tells us:

> Just as each of us has one body with many members, and these members do not all have the same function, so in Christ we who are many form one body, and each member belongs to all the others. We have different gifts, according to the grace given us (Rom. 12:4-6).

My teammates' strengths are a blessing to me, and I must have the commitment to recognize the uniqueness of my family's gifting.

Let me share an example of this in my own marriage. I am excited when I hear people talk about my wife's preaching gift. Since she was a little girl, guest ministers at her church would single her out and encourage her that someday God would use her abilities in a mighty way. Despite this early affirmation, this is not why she preaches so effectively today. Although outsiders were able to discern the gift in her life, it was mostly family members who nurtured her talent.

I was challenged to help develop Michele's potential by a dear friend who sat me down and gently scolded me. He told me that I needed to disciple my wife and that I was the one who needed to help her identify her gifts. Thus I began coaching her, looking for opportunities to cultivate Michele's natural gifts.

I remember hearing her hesitancy before she preached her first few sermons. Following these early preaching opportunities, we spent time discussing her sermons, including her preparation and delivery. I gave honor and value to her speaking gift, and I repeatedly talked about the thousands of women who would someday be blessed by her transparency and forthright manner of speaking. Through God working in me, I was able to help Michele blossom into an international conference speaker.

Acknowledge Your Own Weaknesses

This third factor is often the most difficult to incorporate into a team setting. After all, no one likes to admit shortcomings and deficiencies, but it's still a critical part of team success. Each member must know his or her areas of strength and reliability as well as weakness and vulnerability.

The home should be a place where we can honestly express ourselves. It is a place where it's safe to speak of our inadequacies and where we can rally to cover each other. This does not mean that we conceal our inadequacies in order to deceive, but rather to protect one another. A healthy family should operate like a covering, such as an umbrella. The family umbrella shields the weak person from getting wet. Outsiders who come close enough should see that the weak person doesn't have rain gear on and needs this family umbrella for protection.

However, in an unhealthy family system, everyone stands around the person without an umbrella or raincoat. While they might shield the person and his or her problem from outsiders or public view, they are not protecting him or her from the rain. You see, they protect their reputations instead of addressing the hurting member's need. Further, unhealthy families rarely help the weaker member in tangible ways. For example, these families will set up a false cover for their alcoholic uncle by keeping his drinking problem hidden. Most unhealthy families act like everyone in the family is perfect.

Therefore, it is important to remember that when we acknowledge our shortcomings, we can help one another minimize failures and maximize successes. Then we can fulfill our ultimate goal: That we might grow up to be the household of God who will show forth the praises of Him who has called us out of darkness into His marvelous light (see 1 Pet. 2:9).

GET PRACTICAL: STRATEGY FOR FAMILY DESTINY (S.F.D.)

The preceding factors lay a foundation for a specific plan of action. We must set written goals, which will serve as markers or milestones on our road to success. As someone once said, "A written-down goal, in some way no one yet understands, tends to attract every ingredient it needs to realize it." It is good to break down your vision into bite-size, measurable and time-based goals. One way of doing this is with a tool I call the Strategy for Family Destiny (S.F.D.).

For several years, I used to write down precise, personal vision statements along with annual prayer goals. Ironically, after I meticulously spelled these out, I filed them and forgot about them. Have you done something like that? Don't feel too bad; you are in good company. Lengthy vision and mission statements have become all but useless in the corporate and government worlds. Although these statements are carefully crafted and nicely printed, few organizations carry their visions into action.[5] Our goal is to create a document that is usable, workable and helpful.

Brainstorming Your S.F.D.

I will outline a series of steps that may benefit you when creating your strategic plan.

Step 1: Take a snapshot of your current quality of life. Ask questions of your spouse and your family, such as: How are your communication and intimacy levels? What are your financial policies? Where can you improve in these areas? Remember, at this point, don't get bogged down in trying to fix each problem. Merely identify them for the sake of devising goals.

Step 2: Begin to set some goals. Be bold! Decide where you want to go as a family. What things are most important to you? What things are most immediate? What preparation needs to be made in order to achieve your greatest goals? The goals must be based on faith, but they must also be attainable. The following are questions you might ask yourself and your family.

1. What kind of relationships do we want to develop?
2. How do I want my family to be known?
3. What kind of spiritual legacy do I want to leave?
4. What are my career goals?
5. What are my financial goals?

Step 3: Set a course of action that encompasses the following five elements.

1. *Individual callings.* Each person should identify goals they want to pursue. For young children, of course, these will be simple and may need to be decided by Mom and Dad. Although everyone's purpose is equally valued, sometimes one member's role or career is of more strategic importance. If a mother is the primary

breadwinner—and her income pays for groceries, education and so on—then the family's goals will need to revolve around her work.

2. *The husband-wife relationship.* Michele and I have different needs now than we did when we were young newlyweds. Every couple must spend time talking about those needs, identifying them and considering their implications on the rest of the family. As we create a game plan for the future, we must recognize and respond to the changing needs of our spouses. Goals must be set that will strengthen the marriage, which will then serve as a healthy model for children.

3. *Preparation for the children's future.* It is our God-given responsibility to help our children determine their specific needs. While they're under our roof, we must be equipping them to excel into adulthood. This may require trade-offs, such as choosing private over public education, which could mean delaying other family goals. One caveat: Many so-called needs are nothing more than desires or wishes. I've known numerous couples who have added financial stress—and thwarted worthy goals—because of highly debatable necessities. The only sure way of knowing if you are in need of something is through continuous prayer and devotion to the Lord.

4. *Job realities.* Each spouse needs to look at his or her job assignment realistically. Usually, family financial needs seem to dictate our employment choices. But beyond providing financially, we also must look at the toll a job takes on our time and energy with family. We need to ask ourselves, *What stress and pressure from the workplace spill over to my family relationships?* Once we have evaluated the pros and cons, we can determine if

the job is promoting or postponing the true goals of our household.

5. *Financial goals.* These goals also need to be realistic, leaving room for unexpected challenges. We need to see our planning as a partnership with God's provision. (We'll talk more about this area in chapter 9, which is devoted to finances.)

Creating a S.F.D. Template

Creating your family's strategy does not have to be rocket science, and it doesn't have to follow any particular format. I think it's best, however, if it addresses a few simple questions.

1. Who am I responsible for?
2. What am I going to do?
3. When must I act?
4. Why am I doing these things?

As an example, I have included the Jackson family's S.F.D. This format works for us, but you should modify it for your own family's situation.

JACKSON FAMILY S.F.D.*

Who Am I Responsible For?
1. Relatives
   a. Essie Jackson (my mom)
   b. Evelyn Alexander Booker (Michele's mom)
2. Spouse (Michele)
3. Children
   a. Joni Michele (eldest daughter)
   b. Elizabeth Rountree (youngest daughter)
4. Myself

What Am I Going to Do?
1. Careers
   a. Michele's career

   - Christian education; teacher of children
   - Writer
   - Conference speaker

   b. My career

   - Pastor of pastors
   - Secular corporate boards
   - Adjunct professor
   - Writer (10-15 books)
   - Pastor of local church for at least 10 more years

   c. Joni's career

   - Graduate school of her choice (1 of top 10 scholastically in her field)
   - Coach on life vision
   - Maintain moral purity until marriage
   - Coach about summer jobs

   d. Elizabeth's career

   - Graduate from high school
   - Enroll in prebusiness curriculum
   - Coach to explore training for perceived life vision

2. Finances
    a. Pay off home within 12 years
    b. Buy a smaller summer home to be used as a time-share
    c. Build IRA account to allow slower pace at age 65
    d. Pay for last year of Joni's school
    e. Pay for Elizabeth's college education

3. Relaxation/Vacation
    a. Plan one family vacation a year
    b. Plan one vacation with Michele each year
    c. Practice weekly Sabbath
    d. Follow new rest cycle, with one month out of the pulpit each year
    e. Become an international recreational marathon runner

When Must I Act?
1. Immediate career needs
    a. Michele—get out of office administration
    b. Me—invest in church leaders and staff
    c. Joni—send to training with Generals of Intercession; purpose: LSAT test preparation
    d. Elizabeth—continue SAT training; tutoring in physics

2. Intermediate Needs
    a. Michele—return to school for Ph.D.
    b. Me—accelerate writing
    c. Joni—law school or MBA program
    d. Elizabeth—college

Why Am I Doing These Things?
1. God's Call (see Ezek. 3:1-12; John 16:15)
2. Personal fulfillment/enjoyment
3. Fun through vacation/exercise

*Abbreviated document. The time frame can be enlarged considerably.

Keeping Your S.F.D. Current

Charles Handy tells us, "It is one of the paradoxes of success that the things and ways which got you where you are seldom those things that keep you there."[6] In other words, this means that what worked last year is not guaranteed to work next year. Therefore, we must know how to make changes and transitions within our strategy in order to keep moving in the right direction.

A personal change I made to my S.F.D. happened eight years ago. I had a major health challenge, and God helped me adjust my personal S.F.D. accordingly. I had just turned 40 and was starting to feel tired. I was working hard and was also quite overweight. I went to my doctor who diagnosed me as prediabetic with high blood pressure. He warned me that if I didn't make some major changes, I would have a heart attack or stroke within the next four to five years. I took this news seriously and considered it a life-or-death issue, as my father had passed away just before his 48th birthday.

Naturally, I prayed for God's guidance, and the Lord challenged me to incorporate health and diet changes into my personal vision. I thought, *Boy, you're fortunate to be alive. Why did you wait so long? What's God got to do, give you a personal invitation to obey the rules of the universe?* Ironically, I had felt convicted to lose weight for over six months before the diagnosis. I felt that most people would not have needed a sign from God to address such an obvious problem. However, to my delight, God miraculously healed me! During one of my visits to the doctor, the nurses were saying things like, "We don't know what happened. Your blood sugar was high the other day. Now it's almost normal." It was fantastic news, but I still got the message that I knew I had to lose weight. As the vision for my life changed, I lost nearly 100 pounds. You see, vision creates passion, and passion fuels the engine of accomplishment on our journey.

Here are some additional questions to ask yourself as you consider changes to your vision.

1. Is this new venture realistic? Ask a few of your down-to-earth, pragmatic friends if the idea makes sense to them.
2. If you pursue the thing that's on your heart, will there be a source of income to support you?
3. How will this change your relationship with your spouse and children? What concerns do they have? Will they understand what you are doing and why?

We need to see the strategy we use to achieve our goals like a puzzle. God will work with us to fit the pieces together so that we can see the picture clearly. I encourage you to set up a meeting today with your family to begin the process of creating your own S.F.D. Follow the pattern set here and enjoy fitting the pieces of the puzzle together. Most importantly, remember that your visions and dreams, and those of your family, are part of the Kingdom destiny that God has prepared for you!

CHAPTER 5

THE DEVIL'S DEN OR HOME SWEET HOME?

Strategies for Successful Communication

> *How many a dispute could have been deflated into a single paragraph if the disputants had dared to define their terms.*
>
> Aristotle

Anyone familiar with the American Civil War has read something about the battle at Gettysburg. If the Union had lost at

Gettysburg, the Confederacy would have easily marched to Washington, D.C., and probably won the war. This battle was a turning point, as the Union victory gave the North momentum and confidence.

The battle was actually three days long. More than 51,000 men were killed or wounded, which was approximately 27 percent of the Union soldiers and 40 percent of the Confederate soldiers.[1]

Decisive action in this battle took place on a plot of ground called the Devil's Den, which received its name for a most unusual reason. When pioneers settled, this cave was the home of a huge rattlesnake affectionately known as the Devil. Travelers avoided the cave in order to steer clear of the Devil.

In the battle at Gettysburg, the Devil's Den was a strategic location from where the Union army defended the field against the spirited and unpredictable rebels. In the end, the Union army actually lost the battle at Devil's Den and yielded the ground, but the Confederates paid a high price in both casualties and time. Because of the delay, the North was able to put another line of defense in place and ultimately defeat the rebels.

What does all of this have to do with marital communication?

1. There have been many casualties in the civil war of marriage.
2. You may feel as though you're losing the battle for your family. However, if the communication is handled well and a heroic effort is put forth, you may yet be able to turn things around.
3. I find it ironic that the battlefield was named after a snake, given the fact that the biblical serpent (the true devil) created two major communication problems.

The first problem was between God and mankind. You will recall that Satan declared to Eve, "Did God really say . . . ? (Gen. 3:1). You see, Eve's confusion about God became the basis upon which original sin was committed.

The second communication problem Satan created was between Adam and Eve. After eating the forbidden fruit, they hid themselves from God and later started blaming each other. Even though God had created man and woman to complete each other, the serpent had successfully destroyed the perfect union. Thus, couples have been having communication problems ever since.

CROSSED WIRES

Men and women often run into trouble because of how differently they respond to issues. They have different communication objectives; they speak for different reasons because of differing needs. Many relationships are destroyed because of the misuse and misunderstanding of the unique male and female communication preferences.

If men and women were fully aware of the differences between the sexes and also the different keys to communicating across gender lines, there would be fewer divorces and, thus, fewer alienated

Men and women often run into trouble because they have different communication objectives; they speak for different reasons because of differing needs.

sons and daughters. Unfortunately, as Ralph Waldo Emerson said, "We learn the geology the morning after the earthquake."[2]

Let's prevent the earthquake before it becomes more than a tremor.

My wife, Michele, has the following perspective on communication geology.

> Crossing your communication wires is very easy. Despite the fact that you are speaking the same language, you still might not be communicating. Your life experiences have formed paradigms for you, and you express those paradigms through certain words. Unfortunately, because of your spouse's own life experiences and paradigms, your words trigger mental images for him or her that are often entirely different from what you mean to communicate.
>
> I remember a dialogue that took place early in our marriage that showed the extreme differences in our paradigms. Once when Harry shared the desires of his heart regarding our relationship, I remembered images of *The Stepford Wives* looming large in my mind. (*The Stepford Wives* is a science fiction movie that depicted a community in which free-spirited women were replaced by robots who did whatever their husbands wanted. These robots were warm to the touch, but their hearts were mechanically cold.) I asked several times if he was serious—if he really expected another person to do all that.
>
> In actuality, what he was asking for was a normal relationship, but his words triggered something very different in my mind—prison bars and a jailer. Harry simply wanted a flexible woman who was willing to allow him to lead, care for and provide for her.

As you can see from Michele's story, men and women often *hear* and *say* two different things. I am sure you have had an incident in which a significant relationship was damaged by one poorly handled conversation. This highlights the importance of the words we speak. As Joseph Conrad once said, "There is a weird power in a spoken word, and a word carried far—very far—deals destruction through time as the bullets go flying through space."[3]

Before I go on, let me say that my goal is not to lump everyone together into gender-based stereotypes. I know several married couples who display communication styles opposite to what are considered typical. The man may be good at expressing himself and listening, while the woman may keep everything inside and find expressions of affection difficult.

In your family, the communication barriers and recommended solutions may differ from those in someone else's home. However, an important thing to learn is your spouse's style of communication so that you can eventually reach his or her style. Ultimately, you want your interactions to transform your household from the Devil's Den to Home Sweet Home.

THE MYSTERIOUS MALE

Men often say that women are mysterious—that they can't figure women out—because of women's intuition and the whole feminine mystique. On the other hand, men usually think that their own lives are like an open book.

While men for the most part may be able to understand other men, women can find men every bit as mysterious as men find women. Yes, it's true: Men are both physiologically and psychologically different from women.

This section is aimed at helping wives better understand their husbands. I will discuss four common male "mysteries" and then provide you, as a couple, with a strategy to bridge the gap between your different styles of communication. To help you improve and practice your communication skills, I will give you a homework assignment after each point.

Men Feel Insecure When Women Cry and Show Emotions

Women typically have a broader range of emotions than men do, and they can switch between emotions very quickly. A woman can move from tears of frustration to romance in what seems like a heartbeat. For many men, this flexibility of emotions is seen as flightiness or emotional instability.

Most men believe that their heroic actions or wise words should stop their wives and children from crying. These tears, however, usually emerge because of things that cannot be changed or things men don't understand. Even so, men feel powerless when their words and actions don't solve the problem. Therefore, the more a woman cries in a man's presence, the more unnerving it is for him.

Strategy for Success: Communicate Sensitively. Help your husband understand what is going on in your life. Let's say you are crying because your husband hurt your feelings. Instead of crying, yelling or doing whatever it is that you do when hurt, explain how the circumstances make you feel. By expressing your emotions through words, your husband might become less defensive. If he first understands why you're crying, he can then choose how to respond to your needs. If you don't express yourself through words, he might just think, *I've blown it again.*

Remember that a man's self-esteem is often based on accomplishment—he wants to be your hero! He envisions himself as the caped crusader with near superhuman powers, ready to rescue you from danger. But in reality, your man of valor has no defense when it comes to what you say to him. Your words can affect him the way kryptonite affects Superman—they can render him powerless.

Homework Assignment. If your husband gets nervous when you are emotional, he may ask you more than once what he can do for you. Next time, take him seriously. Sometimes a wife thinks that her husband should automatically know what she needs, but he often truly doesn't understand what she is experiencing. As one friend of mine said playfully, "If he does not have a clue, you should hand out a few at the door."

During the next 30 days, follow these three steps, which will help you provide clues to your husband.

1. Tell him what physical support you need to receive when you're emotionally distraught. For example, Michele would like me to hold her and tell her everything is going to be all right.
2. The next time you are overcome with emotion, remind him to do the thing you'd asked him to do in step one.
3. After the episode is over, show your appreciation by thanking him for his support.

Men Feel Pressured When Women Ask for Decisions

I am not sure why I feel pressure when my wife and other women in my life ask for quick decisions, but I've come up with three underlying theories for my reaction.

1. I don't want to make a bad decision, so I pause and think.
2. The decisions that my wife so faithfully brings to me are *not* the easy ones. She asks me to make decisions that really do require thought, prayer and wisdom.
3. Many men have previously been coaxed into making rash decisions by wives and lovers who have misrepresented the complexities of the decision.

Time and time again, I hear women hearkening back to a promise their men made under duress. They will simply repeat tearfully, "But you promised!" as if to say, "I should have known that you wouldn't honor your word!" A woman may also insist on having an answer right now. In her mind, it may not be a big deal. She may not realize that to a man who fears making a mistake, it is a big deal.

Strategy for Success: Don't Press for Decisions. Early in my family life with Michele, I was frequently off balance. I would feel a wave of anxiety every time I heard the phrase, "We really need to talk!" To me those words usually meant that a long, messy conversation was coming. I knew one of three things would happen: (1) I would be asked to make a major decision; (2) I would be pulled into an emotional area that I couldn't respond to; or, (3) I would be reprimanded for something.

Over the years, Michele learned to give me brief introductions for important conversations. Now she tips me off to the agenda, the urgency of the matter and the time frames involved. She says something like this: "Honey, I really need to talk with you. It will only take 10 minutes. I have got to clear up that bounced-check issue. Can we talk now, or would five o'clock be better for you?" That's more like it—I can deal with that!

The bottom line is you need to know how comfortable your husband is in making decisions. Ask him if the timing is right to discuss a particular topic. Give him an opportunity to think prior to the discussion if he needs to do so. Help him understand the time frame or urgency for his response. But most importantly, learn to wait patiently for his decision.

Homework Assignment. When facing a decision, your husband should know that you value his perspective. Therefore, lay out the issues clearly and give him time and space to work it over in his mind. If you fear he'll drag his feet indefinitely, set a specific time to come back together for further discussion.

For example, let's say you want your husband to come to some decision about purchasing a new home. Over the next 30 days, schedule time to ask him these four questions, one each week.

> Week 1: If we were going to purchase a new home, what kind of financial plan would we have to adopt? A large down payment? A part-time job for me?
> Week 2: What kinds of sacrifices in our budget would we have to make to purchase this house?
> Week 3: What kind of ramp-up time would we need to transition to this property? One year? Two? Five?
> Week 4: Under what circumstances would you work with me toward this goal?

Feel free to adapt this pattern of questioning to whatever unique decisions you face. Approach it slowly, one piece at a time. With time to think about each step, you will find that it's easier for your husband to make decisions, and he won't feel like you're pushing him to make a snap judgment.

Men's Jobs Often Seem to Be Their Primary Focus

For years, Michele thought our relationship was less important to me than my career. However, the truth was that we were simply looking at the same thing from different perspectives. I was working *for* the relationship, while Michele was working *on* the relationship. In other words, Michele worked directly on relationship issues, while I believed that my dedication to my job demonstrated my commitment to the relationship.

Men often have a clear vision of how their hard work in the marketplace will benefit their families. They may have a harder time seeing how a long-term time commitment with their families will reap benefits.

Male reasoning often views relationships as static, immovable objects, while women see relationships as small plants that need cultivation and nurturing. What looks like insensitivity may actually be gender-based ignorance. The good news is that ignorance can be cured with understanding and acceptance of the opposite sex's style of communication.

Strategy for Success: Ask for Support Clearly. Men usually do not understand hints and insinuations. When you need support or reassurance, you have to directly let them know. Women also need to help men understand what that support would look like from their perspective.

When my oldest daughter was in ninth grade, we sent her to a private school on the west side of town. Before long, I began to notice how tired my wife was. When I asked her about this, she explained that she was exhausted from driving the family taxi. All of our family's primary destinations—school, church and home—were in different parts of the city. The worsening city traffic had transformed what used to be annoying short trips into major logistical challenges—not to mention the physical and emotional energy expended in bumper-to-bumper traffic. I wanted to help, but I needed to hear from Michele exactly what she needed from me. That was simple for her to answer. She wanted me to share in the driving duties. So I prioritized getting my oldest child to school while being on call to bring the youngest home. The result was teamwork taxi, and it worked well for us.

Homework Assignment. First, tell your husband how much you appreciate his hard work for the family. Next, clarify in your mind what needs of yours he isn't helping to meet (they might be personal needs, household chores or the kids' needs). Then gently yet precisely let him know what he can do to better help you. For instance, you could create a list of things that you would like done in order to help your family operate more happily and efficiently. If your list has 10 things on it, ask your husband to pick five that he will commit to do. Finally, suggest that you both evaluate how things are going in 30 days.

Men Have a Difficult Time Saying They Are Wrong

This point will come as no surprise to most women. Men usually feel the need to be competent and capable in everything they do. The classic example of a man's aversion to being wrong is the guy driving around in circles in a strange neighborhood—25 minutes late—refusing to stop and ask for directions, all the while shushing his wife.

Women need to understand that men's emotional lives are much more fragile than they let on. Men often come across as cool and in control, while inside they fear looking foolish or inferior. Men believe that admitting a mistake is a reflection of who they are—not just a lack of skills or training in a certain area. The more accepted men feel by their wives, the more vulnerable they can be. It might even lead your man to admit he is wrong.

Strategy for Success: Praise Him Profusely. Your man needs to feel appreciated by you, and positive feedback tells him that he's done a good job. My wife taught me an important communication approach in raising our children—reward approximations. If they try to do what you're requesting, applaud their attempt. In other words, whatever you want more of, openly rejoice about it when he puts forth any effort at all. If your husband takes the time to do something kind, make a big deal out of it.

Homework Assignment. Pick one unique, genuine way to praise your husband daily. Choose a new praise area weekly. At the end of the month, you will have touched on many positive things that your husband has done that are important to you. Here's an added bonus: Expect to get more of what you thank him for.

THE FEMININE MYSTIQUE

As a male "survivor" of living solo with four women (mother, wife and two daughters) for over four years, I feel qualified to speak a word of encouragement to men. No matter how difficult it currently seems to communicate with the women in your family, there is hope.

The trick is for men to overcome the communication hurdles they face when relating to women. In the following pages, I will discuss four unique feminine needs, followed by a corresponding communication strategy and a homework assignment.

Women Need Respect

The average woman puts out a great deal of effort to earn respect, whether it be at home or on the job. The Bible is clear that the woman's desire will be toward her husband (see Gen. 3:16). This means that the praise, approval and respect of her husband and other male authority figures can be a significant factor for her self-esteem. For most women, respect is closely related to acceptance.

> When a woman tries to prove her worthiness through *doing* (in an attempt to be appreciated) she finds herself burning out and never truly feels entitled to respect or support. . . . Through the qualities of her *being*, expressed through heartfelt loving attitudes, her presence can draw out from her man warmth, respect and the desire to serve.[4]

If it seems as though your wife is trying too hard in your relationship, it may be that she doesn't feel accepted or respected by you. For some women, insecurity creates a clingy nervousness that many men find frustrating. On the other hand, women may appear to have a rough-edged devil-may-care attitude when they're not feeling accepted. However, this hardened appearance might also mask a deep need for approval and respect.

It is difficult for the average man to understand that a woman's sense of worth rises or falls based upon his daily response to her. He must honor his wife with words and actions. He must also communicate the important place she has in his life. It is then that she will feel valued and grow in confidence. If these things are not forthcoming from him, she may exert so much effort to achieve respect from her husband that it might become a burden too large to bear.

Strategy for Success: Lavish Her with Praise. If men's affirmation and praise is sincere, it will be healing and uplifting. My esteem for Michele must be made known to her and to other people. I need to praise her not only when I'm with her but also in her absence. The word will get back to her. I have also found that I need to thank her for the specific things she does, explaining why each is important to me. She feels cherished when I do this.

My two daughters also need praise that is anchored in reality. This praise needs to focus on their enduring values and abilities. The tyranny of flawless beauty (face, figure and fashion) can be overwhelming for a teenage girl. So many young women judge one another on appearances—how much or how little they look like the latest pop singer or movie star. This is obviously very limiting and unrealistic; therefore, it is a father's responsibility to help instill confidence by encouraging his daughter's internal qualities.

With this in mind, I choose to compliment my daughters based on their analytic, peacemaking, leadership and academic skills. Although I notice and praise my girls when they look good, I don't want either of them to think that respect or appreciation is based upon outer appearances.

Homework Assignment. If your wife (or daughter) is struggling with respect issues, it is important that you realize something: Her welfare is your personal assignment. No one else will fix her or do something to change her.

This first homework assignment is deceptively simple yet very powerful. Identify the action or task you can perform to show the women in your family courtesy and respect—and do it consistently. Then choose one of the following actions to work on for one month.

1. Demonstrate consideration through your manners (open the door for her, hold her chair and so on).
2. Say thank-you for every act of service she performs.
3. Listen attentively when she speaks and don't interrupt.
4. Consistently tell her how wonderful she is for no particular reason (not just when she cooks your favorite meal).

Women Need to Solve Problems Out Loud

Early in our marriage, when Michele would begin to talk about a situation or issue in her life, I would listen for about five minutes and then say, "Well, maybe you should do this or the other." Her response was, "Let me finish!" Then I would think, *I was only trying to help. I thought she wanted me to solve her problem.* Actually, Michele was just doing what came naturally to her—processing verbally. As H. Norman Wright says:

> Because a woman problem solves out loud, most men either think they've caused the problem or that the woman wants them to solve the problem. It's possible that he *could* fix it, but only if she requests a solution. Most women just want a man to listen and reflect the fact that he heard what she's saying.[5]

In other words, men need to let their wives talk without trying to be Mr. Fix-It. This type of listening is still challenging for me. If my wife sounds angry, I often become protective of her and get angry along with her. If she's talking about a problem with another person, I pick up what I call a secondhand offense against that person. I might see that person the next week and find myself having an attitude problem toward him or her. Why, you ask? Because I am attempting to rationalize and then solve a problem that is hurting her.

Having a negative attitude is not from God, so sometimes after a problem-solving session with Michele, we pray together. This brings emotional closure to our discussions. These prayers help me let go of the issues and place them in God's hands where they belong. After prayer, we move on, both encouraged.

Strategy for Success: Be Verbally Supportive. When your wife is explaining something that is important to her, look into her eyes. Ask questions that will help her explain her feelings: "How did that make you feel?" "What do you think your boss meant by that?" And don't offer an answer unless you are asked.

Then, at the appropriate time, stop and offer a short prayer about the issue. Other specific ways to be a supportive listener are to celebrate verbally good things that she says and to touch her and hold her hand if she starts to show strong emotion.

Homework Assignment. Tell your wife you'd really like to hear about any concern she's currently dealing with. She'll probably be pleasantly surprised. Then surprise her further by simply listening, offering support and not suggesting solutions (unless asked). Point out the positive ways she is dealing with the issue or the positive ways her friends and coworkers are responding to her. Do this at least once a week for the next month, and you'll be amazed at the growth in your relationship.

Women Need Ample Time to Process Change

Just as men require time to make major decisions, women need time to feel their way through potential changes and transitions. Let's say you've been offered a job in another city that meets all of your family's goals and will provide a big raise. You're thinking about the great opportunity, career advancement and extra money. On the other hand, your wife's probably thinking about uprooting the kids, leaving her friends, all the memories made in your current home and many other things that may seem secondary to you.

It's important to give her the time to get a feel for the change, taking into account her emotional identification with the transition. Plus, giving her the freedom to process the idea will help you make a wiser decision for your entire family.

Strategy for Success: Back Off, Man! Most men are rational and pragmatic. If a decision looks good on paper, then what's the holdup? Let's go for it!

Men need to realize that the opinions and perspectives their wives offer are a gift from God. Men benefit greatly when they seek clear input from their wives. On major decisions such as purchasing houses, enrolling in schools, changing jobs or relocating, allow your wife time to come to her own conclusion, and listen open-mindedly as she discusses it.

Homework Assignment. Create opportunities to talk through actual or potential decisions. For instance, if you are thinking about relocating, talk through all of the ramifications—practical and emotional. Next, ask her what things she considers nonnegotiables for a new location: length of drive to work, access to affordable Christian schools, distance from relatives and so on. Issues may surface that will help you avoid long-term problems or wrong choices.

Women Need to Receive Personal Care to Feel Loved

Using the T.R.U.E. relationship paradigm (see chapter 3), I discovered that my wife needs me to express my love for her at frequent intervals in order for us to stay connected. Michele will say to me, "Harry, I'm starting to feel like one of the boys." That's my clue to take action and show her that I love her. In my life there are also two children, a church, a traveling ministry and my hobby (working out at the gym). With all of these commitments, my wife is wise enough to warn me when I'm not connecting with her.

Not long ago, Michele was scheduled to speak at a women's conference one hour's drive from our home. As we discussed this on the phone, I detected a deep tiredness in her voice. I asked if I could have someone drive her to the meeting.

"No," she said, "I really don't have the emotional energy to entertain anyone or make small talk."

I quickly checked my calendar and then said, "Well, how about me? I'll drive you—and you won't even have to make small talk."

That's what I did. I drove her, which allowed her a little time to gather her thoughts and relax before speaking. Rearranging my priorities helped her cope emotionally with the rigorous schedule ahead of her. She told me that my small act of kindness made her feel understood, cared for and supported.

Strategy for Success: Show Love Through Action. To express care for your wife, first verbally affirm your love for her. The typical guy just assumes his wife knows he loves her, but women never mind hearing it again. Tell her, and tell her often.

Attentive listening is another way to demonstrate love. Set a time when you will do nothing but listen to your wife. If a lady feels that it's important for her husband to take the time to hear her out, she will feel genuinely respected. While you are listening to her, keep an ear out for emerging issues. She may give you subtle clues that need to be investigated.

Next, look for opportunities to give personal care to your spouse—pamper her. If you don't know what speaks love to your wife, ask her. She'll be more than happy to tell you. Your wife will feel special when you show your love in specific ways that uniquely speak to her.

All of these actions will multiply the effectiveness of your communication. When a woman feels loved, she feels safe. And when she feels safe, she feels free to share her heart with her man.

Homework Assignment. For the next 30 days, be especially mindful of the suggestions above. Look for specific, tangible ways to express your love. Set aside a time to listen to your wife. She needs to believe that you value her opinion. She needs to feel that she has the freedom to express her feelings, ask questions, make observations and have her own ideas and personality received.

FINAL THOUGHTS

I had the privilege of visiting the Gettysburg battlefield site less than eight months prior to writing this manuscript. The Devil's Den was clearly marked, but I was unaware of its significance at that time. I was moved by how many lives were lost there. The worst part of the Civil War, from my perspective, was how close it came to destroying a great country with a unique ability to impact the world.

Likewise, our families have been endowed with a unique ability to impact the world. I wonder how many families have been lost on the battlefield of poor communication? How many husband-and-wife teams may be at a standoff because they have been operating in the Devil's Den?

Make a decision today to maximize your relationship to the glory of God. If you and I begin to incorporate these principles in our everyday lives, we will experience change in our words and actions. Improving communication is a process, and as we grow in these areas, our relationships will become better than we ever thought possible.

FIGHT THE GOOD FIGHT

Making Conflict Constructive

*There can be no reconciliation where there is no
open warfare. There must be a battle, a brave, boisterous
battle, with pennants waving and cannons roaring,
before there can be peaceful treaties and enthusiastic
shaking of hands.*

Mary Elizabeth Braddon, *Lady Audley's Secret*

In the history of war, there have been occasions when armies
have said to themselves, "Why should everyone get killed? Let's
just get a representative to fight for us." This was the case in the

story of David and Goliath. David's individual contest was designed to decide the fate of his entire nation. In a sense, the unlikely teenage hero fought as a representative of God and man (his nation) (see 1 Sam. 17).

Of course, one-on-one conflicts don't just happen on battle-fields; they occur in homes as well. An unfortunate reality of marriage is that we have fights—or quarrels, disagreements, ani-mated discussions or whatever else you want to call it. One preacher, denying the consequences of verbal sparring matches, called it "intense fellowship." A couple on a Christian radio talk show kept referring to their "contention and discord," which led them to have "fervent tête-à-têtes." Why couldn't they just say they fought and then worked through it?

All of these euphemisms point to the fact that many Christians are uncomfortable with the idea of conflict, especial-ly in marriage. Some people insist that any conflict is wrong and unchristian. To me this is akin to the issue of temptation—it cer-tainly can turn out wrong if we handle it unwisely, but it can also strengthen us if we resist and overcome. Iron-ically, our negative reaction to temptation usually pro-duces something that be-comes the substance of our ministry to others. The apos-tle Paul says that we are to comfort others with the com-fort we have received from God (see 2 Cor. 1:3-4).

> It's imperative that couples air their differences, laying everything on the table, so they can move on in harmony and love.

Therefore, I want to help people get over their fear of conflict so that they see it can be handled constructively. If we work through our conflicts in a healthy, open-minded and fair manner, our marriages will become stronger. We can gain deeper understanding about our mate's perspectives. We can address issues that would otherwise keep us stuck. It's imperative that couples air their differences, laying everything on the table, so they can move on in harmony and love.

Here's Michele's perspective on an argument (I'll call it what it was!) that occurred early in our marriage.

Our most enlightening argument took place when Harry and I were living in Boston while pursuing graduate degrees. Life was hectic, to say the least. Neither of us had the emotional energy to be there for each other. Nerves were continually on edge and tempers flared. Harry indicated that I was not being a wife to him. I responded flippantly and . . . it was on. When we finally returned to our rational minds, we engaged in a two-day discussion that changed my life.

The desires Harry expressed revealed the need to set clear parameters. I was tempted to become intellectually dishonest in order to escape the confrontation and tell him whatever he wanted to hear. Instead, I decided to tackle it head-on.

We had crossed each other previously, but now this crossing would be deliberate. As the discussion progressed, tears were shed and heated words were exchanged, but then came clarity, understanding and decisions that would create more unity in the future.

Most marital fights do not end as positively as the trouble Michele and I had in Boston. The fight we had actually took us somewhere. We ended up with clear boundaries that ultimately resulted in tangible learning.

What is the typical outcome of arguments in your marriage? Do they get resolved or do they linger unfinished for days on end? Do they lead to a peace accord or a cold war? In the following pages, I want to offer some simple, straightforward suggestions for making your marital conflicts constructive.

READY TO RUMBLE

I'd like to use the analogy of a boxing match to describe our marital conflicts. Please don't take this literally—it's just an analogy! After all, the violence and physical aggression displayed in boxing rings have absolutely no place in our homes. What I'm talking about are those verbal sparring matches in which couples jab each other with nasty comments. When tempers flare, couples might retreat to separate corners to fume silently. Poorly fought matches may cause lasting damage both to you and your children; therefore, we need to learn to fight fair.

Let's imagine a sparring match between a Christian couple at an imaginary place called the Marital Square Garden. The once loving couple no longer use their real names. They go by the monikers of Muscles Mannigan, because of the way he muscles his wife to get his way, and Maggie the Manipulator, because she coercively controls what happens in the home. Here's how their world-class title fight might sound on a radio broadcast.

"Ladies and gentleman," the announcer says. "In this corner, standing six foot three inches tall, weighing in at 234 pounds is Muscles Mannigan—all man, all macho. In the other corner, standing at five foot three inches, at 112 pounds, is featherweight Maggie the Manipulator—known for her famous punch, the Honolulu Hook."

Round 1

Muscles Mannigan delivers two left jabs in a row straight to Maggie's head. He growls, "I want to have it out now, right here, until we get this settled!"

Maggie the Manipulator begins to dance. With great skill, she ducks and stops and delivers a body punch just above the belt. "If you say so," she snarls, "but I'm not prepared to share right yet. I need at least a couple of hours to prepare my issues in some kind of logical order."

Round 2

After winning the first round, Muscles begins psychological warfare: "If you think you can dodge this by defusing my temper, you have another thing coming. I took it easy on you in the last round."

Maggie sidesteps her challenging husband, tripping him intentionally. "Now look what you did," she says in mock sympathy. "I'm just trying to discuss this without getting huffy."

Round 3

Muscles closes in for the kill. Everyone knows he's going to knock her out. "I hate what you're going to make me do." He hits her square in the eye.

At that moment, a 300-pound pastor, wearing a black clergy turned-around-collar shirt that barely covers his potbelly, jumps into the ring and hits Muscles from the left.

Maggie the Manipulator's eye is bleeding, but she looks to the other corner and winks her good eye. Then she sorrowfully lifts her eyes to the sky and loudly exclaims, "I hope I can make it. I need prayer support."

Just then, three women wearing T-shirts with the word "Intercessor" in bold letters scramble into the ring. The noise in the arena is deafening. The announcer says over the loudspeaker,

"This fight will be decided by the judges, Shirley Society, Rumor Mill Smith and Dee Relatives."

The Outcome

Who do you think was declared the winner in this bout? This imaginary fight had no real danger attached, but you still might be able to identify with Colley Cibber who said, "Oh! How many torments lie in the small circle of a wedding ring!"[1] Our conflicts are real and we need real help in dealing with them.

Conversely, comedy has the ability to teach us important things. Sometimes exaggeration helps us see true motives behind where we are heading. A story like Muscles and Maggie at Marital Square Garden can give us a humorous warning. I hate to acknowledge that I occasionally feel like Muscles Mannigan, blaming my wife for my unchecked aggression. Fortunately, Michele never pulls Maggie's trick of spiritualizing passive-aggressive behavior. In fact, Michele's honesty has helped me learn many of the tips I want to share with you. And speaking of honesty, if we're going to make conflict constructive, we need to look openly and honestly at our motives when engaging in arguments.

How to Examine Your Motives

How did Muscles Mannigan get so rough and Maggie the Manipulator begin her manipulation? Why didn't they deal with their problems in a civil way? What were they hoping to achieve? Probably each one thought he or she was right and the other was wrong. As the Bible tells us, "All a man's ways seem innocent to him, but motives are weighed by the LORD" (Prov. 16:2).

Motives are underlying goals that steer our actions. While actions are usually clear and definitive, motives lurk in the shadows of our lives waiting to be exposed by the spotlight of truth.

As Christians, we need to let the Lord weigh our hearts. You and your spouse will be fighting a long time if you don't address the issues of motivation.

Your motive as a family communicator should be to serve your loved ones, lift them up and encourage them. You should have the same relationship with your family that a waiter has with you when you go to a restaurant. If I'm a good waiter, then I'm concerned about making your dinner enjoyable. My goal is clear and I have an agreed-upon reward in mind. You don't fear that I am operating with a hidden agenda. In such a situation, neither of us has to use manipulation (Maggie's tool) or pressure tactics (Muscle's approach) to get our way. I am your servant—pure and simple.

> Your motive as a family communicator should be to serve your loved ones, lift them up and encourage them.

The more focused or short-term the relationship, the easier it is to remind ourselves to serve one another. It's harder to remember this in our long-term relationships. We often take those we are most familiar with for granted. This doesn't mean that we are unkind or cruel. It means that we don't serve them or treat them in a way that honors their greatest God-given gifts or allows them to be transparent.

Establishing Clear Motives for Men

Several Scripture passages directly address the roles of husband and father (see Eph. 5:25; 6:1-4; Col. 3:17-23). In these passages, men are clearly called upon to love their wives. Love is more than passion or a special emotional feeling. The Bible coaches men to establish love as the motivation for their actions in the family. According to the Bible, this love must be pure and undiluted.

The problem is that a man's motives are not always pure and undiluted. Three attitudes pollute men's motives: selfishness, bitterness and anger. I believe that these three attitudes are actually progressive stages of the same impure root—self-centeredness. Unchecked selfishness sets a man up for bitterness. And bitterness, when not renounced, paves the way for anger.

The apostle Paul reminds us that the Bible calls a husband to love his wife as dearly as his own body (see Eph. 5:28-29). As this motive is embraced and translated into action, a man begins to mature. Maturity means moving beyond self-centeredness. It means a husband will begin to focus on doing what's best for his wife and family. Self-sacrificing love is the highest form of love. This is true heroism!

If self-centeredness is not eradicated, the second stage of this pollutant, bitterness, can further dilute the love motivation. The pressures of day-to-day problems and making ends meet can cause a man to become irritated with his family's demands. But if men can learn to see themselves as servants of Christ, assigned to serve their wives and family, sacrifices become easy. Paul sums it up nicely:

> Husbands, love your wives, just as Christ loved the church and gave himself up for her (Eph. 5:25).

Establishing Clear Motives for Women

Most people can see through someone like Maggie. We know why she is like she is. Sociology uses phrases like male responsibility and societal dominance to describe her dilemma. After all, Maggie has to do whatever it takes to survive in a male-dominated world.

But does her survival really have to include the serpentine quality of manipulation? Is she really a victim of society? Or is she a coconspirator with an evil system that can make the strongest of men feel emasculated—left with no other response but emotional violence?

The Bible paints Maggie's situation with a different brush than many people in our generation might. Scripture would call her manipulation part of "the mystery of iniquity" (2 Thess. 2:7, KJV). The biblical concept of iniquity includes a twisted character, overlapping problems and hardened sin. When we have been manipulated, we feel used, put down and devalued.

Where does manipulation get its start? There are two things that mark the lives of even the most gifted manipulators: fear and abuse of relational power (influence). What kind of fear am I talking about? You name it or take your pick (see Heb. 2:14-15)!

In numerous passages (see Eph. 5:21-33, Col. 3:18-25, 1 Pet. 3:1-9), the twin problems of fear and the abuse of relational power are addressed. From these and other Scriptures, we can see that women have been given the ability to influence men in a most unusual way. Now, don't laugh, I'm not just talking about the heart palpitations of sexual arousal or the hypnotic affect of romance. Influence is often a connection with people that can go around the normal chain of command or even the spiritual order of things in order to allow them to get their way.

Fear has motivated many women to get off the right path for the most fundamental of motivations—self-preservation. Just like men, women can move from self-centeredness to bitterness to anger. The Bible, however, gives women a personal commandment to which they must adhere. In the context of marriage, the Bible repeatedly calls wives to respect and submit to their husbands (see Eph. 5:22). And it's really difficult to submit yourself to someone if you don't respect them. The challenge for every woman is to submit (rearrange her priorities) to her own husband in the reverential fear of God.

HOW TO HAVE A FAIR FIGHT

The Bible clearly says, "Do not let the sun go down on your wrath, nor give place to the devil" (Eph. 4:26-27, *NKJV*). If we don't bring resolution to our problems, we play into the devil's hand. Our unwillingness to confront problems in a timely manner often leads to escalation or blowups. Therefore we need to be courageous and talk things out. In the words of comedienne Phyllis Diller, "Never go to bed mad. Stay up and fight!"[2]

Let's continue using the analogy of a professional boxing match to illustrate how we should approach these Christian, nonphysical, nonabusive, *fair* verbal sparring matches. I'm going to give you eight rules of the ring, with practical suggestions for positive, helpful disagreements.

Get in Shape

Every athlete knows the importance of conditioning and physical fitness as well as mental toughness. In marital conflict, physical training is replaced by long-term emotional and spiritual endurance. Mental preparation has to do with the renewing or reprogramming of our minds. We actually need to prepare ourselves for successful conflict, anticipating a great outcome. Here are some ways to get in shape before your next argument.

- Lay down some ground rules with your spouse. These may include setting up: a discussion time, a duration time (no more than one hour), the kinds of words that are admissible (no name-calling) and so on.

- Plan what you are going to say and do. Clarify in your mind precisely what the issues are and rehearse difficult statements or assessments. If it's helpful, jot down some talking points.
- Pray ahead of time. If you know you're going to be addressing a difficult issue, ask God for a calm spirit and cooperation to prevail. Ask Him to give you and your spouse words that will promote healing.

Keep Your Eye on Your Opponent

In boxing, it is easy to get distracted. Watching someone in the stands or momentarily daydreaming can get you KO'd in a hurry. You have to keep your eye on your opponent at all times. A very smart fighter will even anticipate his or her opponent's next move.

It is also easy to get distracted in interpersonal conflict. Therefore, you need to keep a careful eye on the things that have the potential of hurting you the most. Keep the following in mind:

- Remember that you are speaking the truth as you see it. Therefore your truth may be open to interpretation. Only the Bible is the ultimate truth.
- Stick to your issues. Don't focus on winning the conflict. Be specific about each issue to help your spouse understand your viewpoint.
- Don't project your problems onto the other person. Jesus said, "Why do you look at the speck of sawdust in your brother's eye and pay no attention to the plank in your own eye?" (Matt. 7:3). In the heat of battle, we're tempted to defend ourselves by pointing out one of our spouse's flaws when, in fact, we have a much bigger flaw we'd like to avoid.

Don't Stall

In boxing, it is possible to dance around the ring without engaging your opponent. However, a lot of time is wasted when a boxer stalls. This tactic will ultimately cause a boxer to lose points in the fight.

Some people refuse to discuss issues because it is beneath them or against their principles—or they're just trying to avoid conflict. But stalling won't win you any points in marriage either. Consider these points:

- Address conflicts in a timely manner. Pretending a problem doesn't exist won't make it go away.
- Don't use indirect communication or hints. Just say what you mean.
- Be prepared to yield if you're wrong. Remember, it's not about you winning the argument. You have won when you have helped the relationship.

Listen to the Referee

The third person in every fight is the referee. Recognized as the authority, he or she serves as arbitrator and judge. Similarly, the only third person who ought to be allowed in the ring of a Christian marital fight is a counselor. Think about these suggestions as you consider who to choose as your referee.

- Pick a counselor both of you can trust. Make sure that the husband is involved in the selection process. (This will be crucial for full participation later.) If you are not familiar with a biblically based counselor, ask your pastor for a recommendation.
- Don't ignore the advice of your counselor or look for a new one simply because you disagree with him or

her. Give the process a chance. It is easy to dismiss directives that are given to address your weaknesses. Trust that the Lord will give your counselor wisdom to help you. If the process comes to a standstill, don't change until an appropriate and logical transition point.

• Don't enlist your friends as counselors. You need a neutral, objective third party. Let your friends remain friends and your counselor remain your counselor.

Watch for the Rope-a-Dope Strategy

Muhammad Ali was a pioneer in fight strategy, and one of his tricks was termed the rope-a-dope. In his 1974 fight with former Olympic champion George Foreman, Ali hugged the ropes for over seven rounds. The pretty boy allowed Foreman to hit him in the body, blow after bone-crunching blow. Ali acted hurt and worn out, but he was actually playing possum and observing Foreman's style. Then, in the eighth round, Ali sprung into action, knocked Foreman down and won the fight.

How does the rope-a-dope strategy apply to our fair-fight approach in marriage? It is a psychological tactic. Therefore, ask yourself, *What is my spouse's real issue in this argument? Why is he or she really responding to me that way?* Often we forget that we're here to fight *for the marriage.* The rush of adrenaline begins to cloud our minds, motivating us to win at all costs. Think through these recommendations.

• Respect your spouse's right to speak out loud. Although word choice and issues may catch you off guard, listen to the words and attempt to understand his or her feelings.

- Don't take everything at face value. What your spouse says may only be the tip of the iceberg. Ask probing questions about your spouse's frustrations.
- Be alert to recurring arguments. Repetitive conflicts suggest that the true issue has never been addressed. If you find yourself arguing about the same thing over and over again, some root problem is not getting resolved.

Don't Hit Below the Belt

Many of the rules that govern professional boxing have been designed to protect the modern-day gladiators from grave injury. During sparring practices, fighters wear protective gear around the head and the loins. Misplaced punches can easily hurt, and many boxers have suffered permanent injury—even death.

It goes without saying that physical aggression of any kind has no place in marriage. But what about emotional and verbal abuse? These wounds are often hidden, yet they can be just as devastating because you know your spouse's most vulnerable, emotional spots. Here are some things to reflect on.

- Remember that you'll be lovers again tomorrow. Your argument will probably be over 24 hours from now, and you'll still wake up or go to sleep with your spouse. Therefore, think about the long-term consequences of your words and actions.
- Remember to avoid saying things that will intentionally hurt your spouse. Don't become so intent on making your point that you say something that will do lasting damage.
- Don't say "you never" or "you always." These absolute statements tend to be inflammatory. Your mate may, justifiably, feel attacked.

Don't Talk Trash

Muhammad Ali, Mike Tyson and a host of other well-known boxers had the habit of taunting their opponents with words. Talking trash may be a part of the game, but sometimes it leads to problems outside the ring. More than one boxer has taken the opportunity afforded by a prefight interview to literally punch his opponent in response to his adversary's trash talking.

We all know the rationale: An aggressive boxer wants to get full publicity, but he also wants to gain the psychological advantage. The logic is that the verbally offended fighter will become uptight in the real fight. The insulting boxer hopes to make his opponent lose his cool in the ring.

In marriage, if we win under the scenario above, it will truly be what's called a Pyrrhic victory. Pyrrhus became king of the little nation of Epirus in 297 B.C. He defeated the Romans on several occasions, but each victory was very costly. After a major victory, in which most of his forces were decimated, he declared, "One more such victory and I am lost."[3] At the end of his life, he had ruined his nation, lost thousands of men and accomplished very little of historical consequence.

In the same way, our loved ones may survive the short-term fight, but the long-term resentment may be too difficult for us to handle. Here are some tips to make sure both parties come out winners.

- Be positive. This includes speaking words of encouragement about the conflict resolution process.
- Stay in control. Colossians 4:6 says, "Let your conversation be always full of grace, seasoned with salt, so that you may know how to answer everyone." Biting your tongue may hurt for a moment, but it could keep the fight from escalating into a full-scale war.

- Keep things in perspective. Don't make a federal case out of everything. The level of your outrage—if there really needs to be any—must match the severity of the problem.

Receive the Judgment with Dignity

Many fights end with the defeated person acting like a sore loser. The infamous words "I was robbed" are often on his or her lips. Sometimes this attitude is a response to a gloating victor. If two boxers fight each other multiple times, their bouts can take on an almost feudlike intensity.

In marriage, we must be humble in both victory and defeat.

In marriage, we must be humble in both victory and defeat. If I persuade my spouse that she was in the wrong, I must do so with grace and dignity. I should refrain from rubbing her face in it. Likewise, if I discover that I was at fault, I need to have the humility to admit it. To achieve a happy ending for your arguments, follow these suggestions:

- Kiss and make up. Most conflicts leave jagged nerves and hurt feelings. Both sides need to forgive from the heart and move on as quickly as possible.
- Celebrate the victory for the marriage, not the individual. If you've won the argument, don't gloat. Look at it as a win for the entire team. Say to your mate, "I appreciate your willingness to work with me on this problem. I feel great about the decision we reached. Thank you for respecting me enough to listen."
- Learn from the process. What did each of you do right that helped to reach a resolution? What could you do better next time?

A FINAL WORD

The truths here have transformed my marriage and my walk with God. I trust they'll do the same for you. As you encounter Christian conflicts—and you know you will—I encourage you to get in shape, commit to fighting fair and work toward resolutions that will strengthen your marriage.

The following chapters will build on the relational skills we have developed so far. Tackling the many problems of parenting, finances and sexuality will be child's play now that we're building on such a good foundation.

HURDLING THE HEDGEROWS

Parenting by Grace

There is only one way to bring up a child in the way he should go and that is to travel that way yourself.

Abraham Lincoln

On June 6, 1944, 11 months before the end of World War II, 90,000 Allied soldiers entered France by land and sea. This event has gone down in history as D day. More than 2 million men would follow, and the Allies would ultimately win the war because of the heroism and sacrifice of those who led the way.

Many soldiers—some still teenagers—underwent intense preparation. Many of these troops trained every day with a five-mile run, rigorous fitness program and, in some cases, months of night maneuvers. As thorough as their training was, it would not prepare them for one important element—the terrain.

Scouts and aerial photography failed to inform the troops about the unique Normandy hedgerows. Once the soldiers got past the beaches, they would have to occupy the farmland beyond. While English hedges were high shrubs that could be jumped on horseback, the Normands used elevated mounds of earth two meters high, with densely planted beech, chestnut or oak trees as hedges. These hedgerows flanked the Normandy fields and protected the roads. It was like having a natural moat around a fortress.

Six thousand German soldiers were arrayed to respond to the Allied attack. In the second day of conflict, an unlikely hero emerged to give the Allies an answer to the hedgerow problem. Lieutenant Waverly Wray was a 250-pound soldier from Batesville, Mississippi. Prior to joining the military, he was a hunter and woodsman who claimed he never missed a shot. Wray was also a Baptist with deep religious convictions. Waverly sent half of his pay "home each month to help build a new church. . . . Some troopers called him 'The Deacon,' but in an admiring rather than critical way."[1]

Drawing on his hunting prowess, Wray began a strategically important foray into the German line at the hedgerows. He killed 10 German officers with a single shot each, and this set the enemy on their heels. He had broken up the German counterattack at Ste.-Mère-Eglise on that morning of June 7. Who would have thought that The Deacon would have been a World War II hero?

Parenting is a lot like battling to take foreign soil. Even with the best planning and training, we're sure to encounter unexpected obstacles and impediments. Like Wray, parents must use their ingenuity, skill and resourcefulness to overcome unforeseen barriers. Fortunately, we do not need to be experts to have victory in parenting. The Deacon had success because of two important things: (1) He used weapons with which he was familiar. We're going to do the same thing by relying on what we've already learned from the Word and principles from our previous chapters; and (2) Waverly had the courage to circum-navigate the hedgerows. We also need courage to circumnavigate the hedgerows of child rearing.

When it comes to raising children, I think of hedges as the developmental stages every boy and girl passes through. Many parents are taken by surprise as a new hedgerow emerges, because the strategy they used in a former stage does not prepare them to surmount the next series of hurdles.

> **Parenting is a lot like battling to take foreign soil.**

Working with the Normand hedgerows was a complex process. The wall-like mounds of earth had a second barrier, trees planted on top of them, not to mention German snipers and artillery hidden from sight. This setup is like the complexities of parenting. If you understand the biology and hormones of developmental stages, it prepares the way for one set of victories. Conversely, if you understand the intellectual and academic ramifications of development, this knowledge will yield another set of victories. A successful Christian parent must push through the developmental hedgerows on many fronts.

I want to suggest to you that the principles and key points presented in this chapter will reduce the parenting challenge back to the simple level that the D day invading force originally envisioned—hedges that could easily be hurdled or jumped while riding. Is such a transformation possible? Yes. That is what's so amazing about grace.

RAISING OUR CHILDREN

When Michele and I had just finished graduate school, she asked me when we were going to have children. Since she initiated the question, I thought I should be positive and encouraging. My enthusiastic response meant something more to her than I intended. She interpreted my words as if having children was one of my greatest desires. To Michele, my answer meant she would have to change her career direction and give up short-term work plans. She was disappointed that she would have to delay using her education and training for years to come. However, Michele was willing to make that sacrifice if that was what I really wanted.

Little did she know that I was afraid of becoming a parent. I was struggling with career choices and the question of how to replenish our finances after two years of privation. Ascending the corporate ladder would require family sacrifices, and I was worried about juggling heavy responsibility between work and home.

It was at this time that my wife came up with something she calls *the primary premise for parenting:* The decision to have a child automatically makes other decisions for you. The event will provide you with another view of the world. Your assignment, should you choose to accept it, is to consciously frame reality for your child, seeking to produce an individual who is capable of fulfilling his or her God-given destiny.

It's true: Parenting has everything to do with the child being equipped to become an effective member of God's kingdom. The Lord has His own agenda that parents must follow, which requires many sacrifices.

This singular decision—to become parents—changed everything for us. Instead of being the typical selfish yuppie couple, our whole worldview had to change. Here is Michele's reflection on our transition into parenthood.

Several questions plagued me about my God-ordained task of motherhood. I was raised in a single-parent family, and my mother had to work because my father had abandoned us. As a result, I fought against all the classic rejection symptoms. I dealt with promiscuity, drug addiction, anger, frustration and violence. I had enough rage to pull a solid oak door off its hinges. I knew that iniquities are often passed on to the children, and I didn't want a child to inherit my nasty temper. However, by the power of Jesus, I knew that somehow the curse could be stopped. I understood there was grace.

After our first child came, I had to pray, "Lord, if this child is watching me, let her see only the good things. Give me courage to address the residue of every iniquitous pattern in my life. Change me so I don't taint this little person." I often cried at the altar because I felt so out of control. I wanted to go back to drugs. I didn't want to be in the Kingdom anymore. I didn't want to do this parenting thing. I wanted to make money. I needed another man! After all, my husband changed his career plan.

I was often buffeted by the enemy. Many nights I stood up and called upon the name of the Lord because the voices inside my head were saying, *You don't have to do this. You have options. You can get a job. You can make money. Somebody else can raise this child!*

As you can see, both Michele and I had to mature in our understanding of life if we were going to be successful parents.

We wanted to raise a child with our values, while leading this person into her unique destiny. Whether parents articulate it or not, we often work at making our kids a carbon copy of our best traits. Unfortunately, with this approach, they become just like us—flaws and all. They seem to catch the negatives so effortlessly. Therefore, every parent needs to tap into God's grace so that the next generation begins a new tradition. As parents, we must realize that God is standing with outstretched arms, offering His grace so we do our job well.

PARENTING BY GRACE

This phrase—parenting by grace—is one that Michele and I coined to describe God's power, which elevates our humble efforts to a higher level. As we obey God's Word, He intervenes with both an external orchestration of circumstances and an internal emotional and spiritual impact upon our entire family system.

Webster's dictionary defines "grace" as "divine love, protection bestowed freely upon mankind, the state of being protected and sanctified by the favor of God."[2] This divine protection is both for the child and the parents. God's grace somehow protects our children from our ineptness. Another definition from *Strong's Exhaustive Concordance* tells us that grace is "divine influence of the Spirit reaching, permeating the living level, facilitating the effectual working of the power of God resulting in His desired change."[3] This definition asserts that grace is an operative power that gets inside of man, deals with the issues of his life and causes change according to God's plan.

All of this is great news, but there is one contingency: God energizes and transforms only willing vessels. As our character is transformed, we will become useful vessels and grace will enable us to be the parents the Lord desires. This grace will help us hurdle the hedgerows and overcome obstacles.

Pass It On

Michele mentioned the anger she had developed while growing up, and part of this was caused by a mother who criticized and nitpicked. She would constantly badger Michele: "Couldn't you do better than *that*? Why did you cut your hair?" Consequently, Michele developed deep resentment toward her mom and, in fact, didn't like being around her.

One day during the summer before Michele left for college, her mom called Michele into her room and she apologized. The Lord had spoken to her and made her realize that she had made Michele angry by riding her all the time. Michele's mother began to weep. It powerfully impacted my wife. This exchange was one of the major events God used in bringing Michele to salvation. The Lord loved this teenage girl enough to deal with her mother. Michele was amazed at two things: (1) God's compassion and her mother's obedience; and (2) If her mother could change, Michele also knew that she could change. As we reflected on that experience and many others, we realized that promoting grace meant we could receive help from God and pass it on.

> God's design is for parents to grow with their children and tackle the problems of each successive season.

The basis for parenting by grace is a balanced application of the Word. John 1:14 states that Jesus was "full of grace and truth." Many believers are so zealous to obey the Word of God that they end up with a legalistic adherence to rules without understanding the heart or spirit behind the words. At the other extreme are parents who give their kids *grace* to the point of *disgrace*. Although God is love, He is also a God of order and justice. Children who are able to follow rules and obey authority have usually been taught to do so at home. Disobedient children have often been raised with an imbalance in grace and truth.

Know the Times
Scripture provides a picture of the kind of parents we're supposed to be. In 1 Chronicles 12:32, we read that the sons of Issachar "knew what Israel should do, and they knew the right time to do it. Their relatives were with them and under their command" (*NCV*). Like the sons of Issachar, we need to understand the times in which we live. We must also perceive the issues that confront our children at each developmental level and act accordingly. God's design is for parents to grow *with* their children and tackle the problems of each successive season.

For example, when our daughter Joni was four years old, she suddenly wanted to be useful and helpful. One day, I took her to the grocery store with me. Returning home, we pulled into our long gravel driveway, and I prepared to carry the shopping bags into the house by myself. Though I knew Joni was going to ask if she could help carry the bags, I was ready to tell her no. Our house had steep steps leading to the front door. A few weeks before, she had fallen headfirst from these stairs while under my care. By God's mercy, Joni had only scratched her nose, but she could easily have broken her neck. At that time, I rejoiced not only because God had protected my daughter from harm, but also because He had protected me from Michele.

Then came Joni's predictable question, "Daddy, can I help?"

I tried to distract her by giving her a different assignment. The heavy door of the Oldsmobile was propped open after I had removed two bags from the back seat, so I said, "Okay, Joni, you can help by closing the door. Be careful—just push it."

"Daddy, I can't do that," declared Joni.

"It's okay, honey," I insisted, "just push the middle of the door." When she made no movement toward the car, I tried one final exasperated urging, "Really, Joni, you can do it. Just push the door slowly!"

Joni looked so serious with her brow furled, observing the door and the bags I was carrying. Finally, she said, "Daddy, I can't. I'm just a child!"

I stopped and laughed, almost dropping my bags. Here my daughter had been badgering us with requests to help all day long. Then, when I finally suggested something she could do, she didn't want the assignment.

This story underscores the dance of development our children go through. Helping little people negotiate a big world filled with challenges, uncertainty and dangers is not an exact science. Becoming aware of what my daughters were facing was a challenging process for me. Time and again I had to remind myself that God had given me the job of raising our children for His sake. This mind-set catapulted me to higher standards: to discover the capabilities and calling of each of my girls. I realized that we were simply caretakers of these special people God had given us.

UNDERSTANDING NEW SKILLS FOR NEW STAGES

In the following pages, I want to describe eight developmental stages, or hedgerows, for our children. I will discuss each stage's unique physical and emotional needs and explore communication keys, relational needs and the kind of grace parents need to follow.

Each developmental stage creates an opportunity for children to mature and grow in three ways: physical, emotional and spiritual. Each stage requires parents to recognize its specific dynamics. The following list acknowledges the kinds of grace-filled skills we must cultivate to move successfully through each hedgerow.

Stage of Development	Grace Needed
Prenatal (conception to birth)	Caring and Acceptance
Infancy (0 to 1.5 years)	Caring and Patience
Toddlerhood (1.5 to 3 years)	Caring and Nurture
Preschool (3 to 5 years)	Caring and Competence
Childhood (6 to 9 years)	Commanding with Love
Adolescence (10 to 12 years)	Communicating and Listening
Teenage (13 to 15 years)	Coaching Through Change
Late Adolescence/Adult (16 to 19 years)	Counseling with Respect

Prenatal (Conception to Birth)—Caring and Acceptance

Samuel Butler once quipped, "Parents are the last people who ought to have children."[4] We may laugh at this statement, but with a dash of irony. After all, most parents' idyllic thoughts of a warm, cuddly child are combined with the fear of the awesome responsibility of raising a child.

The physical and emotional challenges for a pregnant mother can seem overwhelming, and the mom-to-be must take special care of herself and the child she carries. Of course, the prospect of having a new baby presents some challenges for dads too. During Michele's first pregnancy, I was concerned about her and the baby. I went through sympathetic morning sickness. I had a queasy stomach, often unable to hold down my own food. Imagine both of us rushing to the same bathroom at the same time!

Unfortunately, Michele spent a great deal of her second trimester alone. I regret that business-related travel kept us separated during those critical months. She began her pregnancy in

Ohio, was separated from me geographically for nearly three months and finished her pregnancy in Corning, New York. My emotional battles were nothing compared to her battles.

I learned that everyone in the family should help mom accept the pregnancy and prepare for this new life. It should be a time of nurturing, encouragement and care. Lack of affirmation or indifference by the husband often sends the wife into depression. That's why men must be involved and supportive. As the father cares for the mother-to-be, she passes the warmth and acceptance to the living person within her.

Communication Keys. Many couples get so caught up in preparing for the blessed event that tension and pressure increases in the household. Although preparation is important, it can subtly shift the focus from the true parental preparation (a loving heart and nurturing environment) to that which Madison Avenue and the retail industry feel are the essentials for an infant. Additionally, many women have unspoken fears about the longevity of their marriage and their ability to really be a good mom. Therefore, this is a great time for couples to dream about their long-term life vision.

Finally, a husband would do well to simply be there physically for his waddling woman, while reassuring her of his love and commitment. He would also ease her emotional and physical distress by talking much about his wife's radiant beauty.

Infancy (0 to 1.5 Years)—Caring and Patience

When Joni and Elizabeth were babies, they needed safety and security. We lavished them with affection and tenderness. Michele talked to them and helped both of them develop pleasant personalities. She also began to help them accept the word "no" by gently saying, "No, no, not for Joni" or "No, Lizzie." By the time our girls were 18 months old, they had calm, quiet demeanors. They even looked like they were *listening* to the sermon in church (but maybe that was just a preacher's wishful thinking).

There are four things I remember from this phase.

1. The workload around the house increased dramatically.
2. Relieving my wife from baby duty was often necessary.
3. Michele longed for adult conversation after the baby was put to bed.
4. The mothering instinct brought about a total personality change in my wife.

At this stage, fathers can make a powerful contribution by participating as much as possible. Research has shown that children manage stress much better during their school years when their dad is "present, accounted for, and playfully involved" in the first eight weeks of their lives.[5] What's more, children's mental and motor development is higher if their fathers have played with them during the first six months of infancy.

Communication Keys. Many parents consider the early days of infancy as glory days. Everyone stops to look at the cute bundle. The attention can make even the shyest mom feel like a movie star or folk heroine. These high affirmation levels are significant to the parents because children at this stage rely totally on adults. Babies seem to pick up on their parents' state of mind. Security and trust are instilled by your smiling presence, cuddles, soothing songs and personal warmth.

Toddlerhood (1.5 to 3 Years)—Caring and Nurture

Around 18 months, children begin to express themselves in language. Children at this age are also now walking, jumping and moving quite freely. The emotional needs of the toddler begin to emerge. This 18-month-old is trying to become independent.

This child has a mind of her own! is the sudden realization of many mothers. Self-awareness should not become selfishness. Therefore, sharing has to be taught, first from an emotional point of view and then as a spiritual virtue.

Communication Keys. At this stage, kids' favorite word becomes "no!" Working through these nos is a tiring yet necessary process. Some people feel as though children are just repeating the word they've heard so often. There may be some truth to this, but they are also exercising the need to express their own uniqueness. Be encouraged—this is just a phase! This too shall pass.

Identify specific behaviors to praise the child for as he or she acquires skills and individuality. For example, "Oh, that's wonderful when you help Mom that way! You're really growing up." The fact that sharing with others is so difficult shows me why these affirming words are so important. I'm also convinced that from the point of view of T.R.U.E. relationships, the toddler is entering a stage when trust is a major lesson. Therefore, we must be consistent and trustworthy—we must do what we say. If we make promises, we must keep them.

I recommend three things during this parenting-by-grace season in regards to discipline.

1. Prioritize physical safety. Be prepared to deal with your child strongly about safety issues. From child abuse to moving vehicles, danger is all around your toddler. Be protective.
2. Decide the specific tasks your child can do. Picking up toys, getting ready to leave the house and mealtime duties are things a toddler can accomplish. Remember, he or she needs to feel independent. Let him or her practice independence by doing these tasks, and then praise him or her for a job well done.

3. Work on teaching your child how to say no nicely and respectfully, so he or she learns to make statements that are grace filled.

Preschool (3 to 5 Years)—Caring and Competence

This phase of life is marked by an increase in learning as children ask question after question. The good news is that preschoolers can also tell stories, enjoy books and use their imagination. It is a time when parents can develop their child's creative thinking. You can also ask questions and make up stories that begin to build reasoning skills.

During this phase, kids start grasping deeper aspects of faith and God, so you can begin to explain spiritual concepts more fully. Also, these young, uncluttered minds have an amazing ability to learn Scripture verses, songs and stories. Kids should also learn about God's protection and provision. My wife's key verse for our kids was "When I am afraid, I will trust in you" (Ps. 56:3).

Teaching our children how to pray was the greatest spiritual-growth opportunity for our kids. When Joni was four years old, she became convinced that she wanted a sister. Michele and I did not know that she had requested the prayer of all the Sunday School classes at our church. One day, Joni announced to me, "I'm going to have a sister, and her name is going to be Elizabeth." Her statement was made with such authority that it was intimidating.

Michele and I had determined to wait before having another baby. The only way we could appease the insistent Joni was to tell her that if we did have a baby girl in the future, we would name her Elizabeth. In spite of our plans to wait, my wife became pregnant within a month of Joni's declaration. The doctors informed us during the third trimester that our baby was going to be a boy. About four weeks before Elizabeth was born, we finally convinced Joni to accept the fact that she might have a brother. But the surprise came to all of us informed adults in the delivery room when a little girl was born. It was no surprise to Joni. From the first day of Elizabeth's life until now, there has been a special bond between them. It began in the prayers of a four-year-old.

Communication Keys. From a T.R.U.E. relationship perspective, it will be beneficial to emphasize respect in your training. Parents must respect the validity of a preschooler's need to be an individual, and the child must be taught to respect others. Children will be able to see our respect as we apply the grace of caring to them.

We must also promote a sense of competence in their lives by giving them simple, age-appropriate assignments and then praising them for their efforts. For example, have them put away their toys every day at the same time and then praise them for their obedience and organization. Additionally, showing off in public or using bad words should not be tolerated. My kids would show off in public even though in private they had many fears and self-esteem issues. Our house rule was: If you sin in public, you get corrected in public. If you sin in private, you get corrected in private. This stopped a lot of the embarrassing behavior in public places.

Childhood (6 to 9 Years)—Commanding with Love

At this phase, children feel compelled to test parental limits. This is normal and natural, and it helps kids learn boundaries. Kids can excel in the arena of developing a conscience, with its inner mechanism of confirming right over wrong. The challenge of encouraging our primary school student to grow academically, spiritually and emotionally can be quite a balancing act.

This stage is a time of commanding, which means the parents give clear direction with few choices. This establishes boundaries for the child's independence. It is helpful if you reinforce the foundations and establish what you want to happen in the future. We found that three things needed to be instilled in our kids at this phase.

1. Respect for authority
2. Obedience to direct commands
3. Attitude development and control

We taught our girls lessons on how to be angry without being explosive and negative. Socialization without selfishness was another big challenge, as our kids had to be taught to be generous, compassionate and caring. Christian attitudes had to be developed by instruction and command. If our daughters pouted too much, we had to discipline them. This discipline has had its fruit in the character our daughters display today.

Communication Keys. The foundation of this phase must be vigilant understanding. For example, Elizabeth fought for respect during the primary school years. As the youngest, she had a need to be heard and acknowledged. Unfortunately, the pressures of being a preacher's kid also weighed heavily upon her. It is not easy to attend a school and church where one parent was the principal of the school and the other the senior pastor of the church. The jealousy of other kids and expectations of teachers put Elizabeth in a bind. Unlike some children, her sense of fairness was overdeveloped. Michele and I helped her through this time by focusing on her uniqueness and acknowledging her special traits.

At this stage, discipline must include clear rules and fairness. It is easy to overestimate the understanding and attention span of the average child. Punishment should be meted out in a timely manner while the memory of the infraction is still in the child's mind. We found it important to ask our girls why their privileges were being taken away. If they could clearly articulate why they were in trouble, we knew they understood the cause and effect of their behavior.

Parents need to articulate their expectations clearly. We must let our kids know that we expect the chore to be done—and when and how. If necessary, we should demonstrate how it should to be done. The process is: (1) we demonstrate, (2) they watch, and (3) we do it together. Finally, we need to evaluate the progress and help them make adjustments. This helps the child remain teachable and enjoy a greater likelihood of success.

Adolescence (10 to 12 Years)—Communicating and Listening

In adolescence, communication becomes key to our success. Pubescent children are very insecure. Despite this insecurity, they begin to challenge authority more than ever before. As parents, we have to help them establish the difference between right and wrong. Talking with our kids becomes critical for establishing a frame of reference for their decisions.

One challenge in this preteen phase is the awakening of sexual desire. It is well documented that physical and emotional desire for the opposite sex occurs much earlier than it did a few decades ago. Therefore, values about dating or courtship have to be discussed and made clear. You and your spouse must come to a solid agreement about guidelines for dating and opposite-sex friendships and you must remind your child of them often.

Role models and heroes are needed during this phase of life. Steer your kids toward books, movies and television shows that present people whose lives are worth emulating. Seek out mentors in your church or community who will be a positive influence on your children.

Communication Keys. It's likely your adolescents will challenge your family standards. Your kids, like mine, will want to inform you about the rules at everyone else's house. We've got to avoid a laissez-faire approach to rules. The tension usually comes from trying to keep the rules relevant and intact without breaking kids' spirits.

Acceptance is a primary concern for this age group. Adolescents want to fit in. Therefore, if we have not framed their reality and given them a sense of security within the family, they will try to find it someplace else. For guys, this often means proving themselves—perhaps acting macho and tough—to win the admiration of friends. Young women may try hard to join the most popular groups and the most admired clubs. Many parents of adolescents feel replaced by their kids' peer group, but young people still want Mom and Dad involved in their lives. Keep the lines of communication open.

Parents need to look at the unique gifts of their children and make a demand on those gifts. This will build self-esteem and self-confidence. We also have to set clear examples for them in how we live. Finally, clear boundaries of right and wrong will give them the kind of personal job descriptions they need to be successful.

Teenage (13 to 15 Years)—Coaching Through Change

Teens need encouragement to grow as individuals. At this stage, parents no longer serve as "the general"; we transition to coach. A great athletic coach looks objectively at the ability of a player, pointing out ways to excel and develop. The coach does not actually play in the game, of course, but he can help the players make the most of their opportunities. During the teen years, we coach our kids to be deprogrammed from the world and every-day peer pressure when they come home. And there are life skills yet to be taught—money management, relational skills, work ethic and so on.

Teenagers experience an accelerated sexual awareness and maturation. There is a corresponding intensity of interest in the opposite sex. The strong pull from the birds and the bees part of the brain is combined with a need for extended periods of physical rest. This is not laziness; it is simply the way the body adapts to the need for growth and change. In the early teen years with Joni and Elizabeth, I became critical of their busy schedules during the week and apparent laziness on the weekend. I found out the hard way that a lack of rest can create a moodiness that I liked less than their Saturday sleep-ins.

Teens also need to learn to filter out cultural deception, humanism and all kinds of faulty philosophies. Questioning is normal as they develop a strong voice for fairness. The question for all teens to ask is this: "In a world where everything is considered relative, whose standard can we use for fairness?" The way they learn is through open dialogue and discussion with a coach.

My daughters were famous for pointing out my hypocrisy and inconsistencies. Ironically, these dialogues around values and actions were healthy. If teens go to their room, put on their headset, turn on their TV and shut you out, you cannot deprogram them. We must establish a line of communication so we can coach them.

When Joni was in the eighth grade, I was shocked that she began to be defiant. More and more I felt like an outsider. She had switched schools, and I didn't realize she had befriended a lot of girls whose fathers had abandoned the family. According to Joni, none of her close friends had dads telling them what to do and complicating their lives. Once during a heated argument I blurted out, "What do you have against me? What have I done to make you treat me this way?" She stared at me blankly and then started to weep. Somehow I had stopped talking to Joni. I had lost connection with her.

Fortunately, Michele was able to help Joni understand that having an intact family was God's will. I had to address three problems in our relationship: (1) I had stopped talking to her friends; (2) Our personal time together had been squeezed out by other things; and (3) I had forgotten how important peer acceptance was at that age. Finally, as I prayed about the situation, the Lord seemed to direct me to a private school with excellent academics. Despite Joni's resistance, we enrolled her there the next semester. Her attitude was totally different in less than six months after the change.

Communication Keys. Since social acceptance is of utmost importance to teenagers, parents need to provide a safe relational place to which their kids can retreat. A church youth group, sports team or other clubs can have the tendency to become an extended or surrogate family. Therefore, we've got to know who our kids are hanging out with and what their families are like.

My daughters needed respect during this time. Unfortunately, the kind of respect they sometimes asked for was exemption from the family's rules and values. Kids need as much structure as we can give them. I found that as I explained why rules existed and enforced them consistently, the girls came to adopt our values as their own.

I also had to apply the grace of expressed love to our relationship. I encourage you to lavish praise on your kids during this difficult season. Hugging, touching and verbally communicating love will help your teens have a sense of value and acceptance. This will keep boys and girls from feeling such emotional need that they seek peer attention at all costs.

Late Adolescence/Adult Stage (16 to 19 Years)—Counseling with Respect

The late adolescent period is a time in which our children still seem young and inexperienced to us. They appear to be adults trapped in a young person's body—or a kid trapped in a big person's body. There's often a mismatch of appearance and maturation.

The kids themselves are probably most confused of all. Maturity gaps are manifest in so many areas. One of our biggest goals should be to help them choose sexual purity. Once a young person becomes sexually active, Pandora's box has opened. It's often difficult to put sexuality back in its proper place. (The latest statistics say that 50 percent of teenagers are sexually active at 16 years old.)[6] A second major choice is life without substance abuse. The problems of liquor and drug experimentation are clear, but even kids from the greatest backgrounds can make choices that lead to years of pain.

Additionally, our children shouldn't leave home until they're ready to go. Just because many parents say "You've got to go at 18!" doesn't mean they're prepared to do it. This age requires parents to assume the role of a counselor who presents options and encourages the training process. Even if kids leave home, parents must be available for advice. Our counsel can help teens stay focused on the right priorities and see the long-term consequences of their actions. As our children grow up and have their own kids, we cease to have direct authority. But we still have something very valuable—influence.

Communication Keys. One of the difficult tasks for parents is loosening the reins or letting go of the child. Parents are often more accommodating of their children's maturity in theory than they are in practice. Late adolescence requires a major change in both parental attitude and practice. If we have vestiges of authoritarianism and control, kids pick up on this and begin to feel as though their changing into young adults is being devalued.

From a T.R.U.E. relationship perspective, respect must be cultivated. Learning to ask appropriate, nonintrusive questions is a great skill to master. Two things need to be accomplished at the same time. First, we find out what's going on in our children's world. Second, we show them respect by listening.

It's also important that we affirm our confidence in our children's gifts and core values through praise. Praising them in the presence of their peers and other adults can help cement their understanding and commitment to the things that we prize most highly about them.

CONCLUSION

The major temptation in child rearing is to try to program your kids so they'll be just like you instead of a disciple of Jesus Christ. Each development phase of childhood offers its distinctive problems. As we saw in the battle for Normandy, it takes a unique soldier, like Waverly Wray, to make a difference. If we truly want to parent by grace, we must remember that our goal is to diligently provide a safe terrain for our children to grow. We must also dare to believe that God will help us increase in grace as we disarm enemy fortifications at each hedgerow in the growth of our children.

An ancient African proverb declares that it takes a whole village to raise a child. This may be true, but the primary teacher and vision caster is found in the home. In the day of dual-career families and hour-long commutes, it may take a church, grandparents, a Christian school and other community dynamics to mold your child. Ultimately, however, it is still the hand that rocks the cradle that rules the world. This phrase used to generate images for me of a woman alone at the cradle. I now see a picture of a husband and wife—standing together. God's grace will empower you to overcome both your unique internal and external struggles. By the time our kids leave home, both parent and child will reflect more of the light of Christ to the world.

CHAPTER 8

A PRIZE WORTH PURSUING

Making Sex in Marriage Magnificent

*For lovers, touch is metamorphosis. All the parts
of their bodies seem to change and seem to become
something different and better.*

John Cheever, "The Bus to St. James's"

In 1808, Napoleon Bonaparte, one of the greatest military
strategists of all time, eyed the nation of Spain as a prize he
simply had to have. Known for his hubris, Napoleon had
presumptuously overrun this proud nation with his troops. The
Spanish army would prove brittle on the battlefield and unable

to defeat the flashy French army. Napoleon's plan was to impose his brother as the king of Spain and create a French ally. A quick victory would have freed up Napoleon's forces for action elsewhere in Europe.

Unfortunately for Napoleon, he was soon lured into a costly guerrilla warfare or terrorist-like atmosphere with atrocities and reprisals. The armed forces, the Spanish people (supported by the offshore British navy) and the difficult terrain are what defeated Napoleon. For the next six years, the nagging situation, called the Peninsular War, was like an ulcer—an open and painful wound. This unconventional war drained time, resources and focus. Thus the Spanish Prize became the Spanish Ulcer, according to historians. The Peninsular War ended just one year before the legendary confrontation of Napoleon with Wellington at Waterloo.

In a similar way, sexuality can be one of the greatest aspects of marriage—or a nagging source of contention. Many spouses underestimate the complexities involved in making marital sex excellent. Our pride, like Napoleon's, can push us into poorly calculated situations. For many, sexuality becomes an ulcer that brings more discomfort than comfort, more anguish than excitement. This open wound can often destabilize a marriage that should be happy and harmonious.

Discussions about sex can cause us to blush or chuckle nervously. But since God created sex, and because it is such an important part of marital intimacy, we should discuss it in an open, honest, straightforward manner. In the following pages, I will address some myths about sexuality and answer frequently asked questions from a biblical perspective. With the myths debunked and addressed, we can use the skills we have learned about communication, T.R.U.E. relationships and fighting fair to create the kind of sexual relationship with our spouse that is the prize instead of the ulcer.

The imagery of a Napoleonic war provides an illustration of what *not* to do. We remember Jesus' words in John 10:10: "The thief comes only to steal and kill and destroy; I have come that they may have life, and have it to the full." The three acts of Satan identified here are significant as we look at the arena of sex. The thief, like an invading army, wants to steal, kill and destroy our sex lives and our sexuality. Satan wants to use what God has created and employ it for his own purposes.

If Satan cannot steal or commandeer our sex lives, he desires to kill (remove life from) our sexuality. There is energy and vitality in marriages that have healthy sex as part of their foundation. The enemy will attempt to damage, distort or destroy sexuality in marriage to the extent that we miss God's intended blessings.

MARRYING FOR ALL THE RIGHT REASONS

Humorist Art Buchwald said, "I don't know whether it is normal or not, but sex has been something that I take seriously. I would put it higher than tennis on my list of constructive things to do."[1] All kidding aside, everyone would agree that sex is an important aspect of marriage. This statement begs the question, Just *how* important is it? A study by George Barna revealed that 60 percent of people marry because they want companionship. An additional 24 percent get married because they want to give and receive love. Ironically, only 3 percent of the people polled got married in order to have frequent sex.[2] Sex may be an important aspect of marriage, but it is one among *many* important aspects.

Here's something else interesting about Barna's study: 60 percent of those surveyed believed that the Bible has nothing to say about sexuality.[3] These respondents couldn't be more wrong. The Bible is filled with stories about red-blooded people as well as important principles about satisfying sex. The high rate of adultery and promiscuity in America shows that we have something very wrong in our thinking. We desperately need help—biblical help! Yet most people, including many Christians, are ignorant about what God's Word has to say about sex.

Many secular studies confirm Barna's conclusions. These studies clearly show that if you live with someone prior to marriage, you most likely will *not* have a happy marriage. This means that disobeying the biblical standard of *not* cohabiting prior to marriage can cause marital dissatisfaction or failure. Similarly, only a small percentage of those who engaged in sex prior to marriage had happy, trusting marriages. The truth contained in the Bible works whether or not we understand the commandments and principles. Disobedience to God's original design for sex has caused it to lose its luster. Yet we can rediscover the divine purpose of sex.

LEARNING WHAT THE BIBLE SAYS ABOUT SEX

Some people are surprised to learn that there are steamy passages in Scripture, such as Song of Solomon 7:6-10.

> How beautiful you are and how pleasing, O love, with your delights! Your stature is like that of the palm, and your breasts like clusters of fruit. I said, "I will climb the palm tree; I will take hold of its fruit." May your breasts be like the clusters of the vine, the fragrance of your breath like apples, and your mouth like the best wine. May the wine go straight to my lover, flowing gently over lips and teeth. I belong to my lover, and his desire is for me.

Can you believe this passage is in your Bible? There's also the writer of Proverbs who says,

> May your fountain be blessed, and may you rejoice in the
> wife of your youth. . . . may her breasts satisfy you always,
> may you ever be captivated by her love (5:18-19).

Another translation uses the word "ravished" instead of "captivated." What do these passages tell us? Clearly the Bible is in favor of marital love that is exciting, intense and passionate. A euphoric quality to sex should exist in our marriages that has no negative side effects. There do not have to be disclaimers stamped on the packaging of the gift of sex. However, there should be strict adherence to the detailed instructions written in the owner's manual—the Bible.

As human beings, the goal of our *sexual* intimacy is to enhance *emotional* intimacy. The physical pleasures of sex, if viewed correctly, lead to more intense emotional closeness with our spouse. Sometimes as we go through the mechanics of sex, we disconnect from its purpose and wind up having wonderful feelings that fall short of the intimate connection of two spirits that God intended. Many married people have become bored with sex because it lacks something. That something is called emotional intimacy.

Like many other couples, Michele and I have had our share of problems in the arena of sex. Listen as Michele offers a woman's point of view.

> Sex begins in the mind of a woman. It can be a passing
> thought that triggers a romantic fancy or a fragrance
> that calls forth the memory of a tender moment.
>
> A bubble bath, a special meal, soft lights, music, scented sheets, that special outfit that drives him mad—all the
> ingredients that the "love doctor" prescribed are present.
> What could go wrong? Invariably, I would be in the mood
> and he would not or vice versa. It took a while for us to get
> on the same page, and sometimes we still aren't.

Personalities play a major role in sexuality. As a choleric woman, I am a night owl, sometimes spending the entire night doing personal projects. This wreaked havoc in our marriage and caused a tremendous amount of conflict. Attacking the issue head-on proved to be the best solution. Some of our most heated arguments centered around sex and sexual fulfillment. If I didn't come to bed, it could appear as rejection, manipulation or withholding sex. But the intention actually was to finish a project. A lack of communication or getting the signals crossed perpetrated an unintentional insult.

You can see from Michele's story that we had some work to do in our sexual relationship. As someone once said, "Marriages are made in heaven, but we are responsible for the maintenance work."[4] The rest of this chapter will troubleshoot our relationships with a little preventive maintenance in the arena of sex. We must keep our eyes on the prize and win the battle for emotional and sexual intimacy.

UNDERSTANDING DIFFERENT PERSPECTIVES

How can we improve a troubled sexual life? I want to remind you that everything flows out of emotional intimacy. Many people are living as if they were roommates and not husband and wife. If you and your spouse have not been intimate for months, you are living with a ticking time bomb. Often we are not honest in our communication about our sexual intimacy. Instead of dealing with problems or needs in a timely manner, we just hope it all works out okay. We let issues fester until sexual intimacy is diminished.

Romantic Love

I'll never forget a major argument Michele and I had outside a theater one night. She turned to me with a romantic look and said, "Let's fall in love again, the way we were when we were younger." Instead of feeling flattered, I felt hurt. I thought to myself, *We are in love. That's why we're out on a date. That's why I am making all this effort.*

Men tend to think in black-and-white terms. They are either close to someone or they are not. In regards to their wives, they are either in love or they are not. Women do not have this all-or-nothing perspective. They think in terms of degrees—a continuum of closeness and feeling in love (anywhere from cold to hot). The key for many men is to touch their wife emotionally each week. As often as we want to touch our mates physically, let's make sure that we touch them emotionally first and foremost. What my wife was saying to me on our date was that I had touched her emotions, but there were many times I hadn't tapped into her same vision of closeness and acceptance. Without understanding more about her personal concept of what it meant to be truly loved, the romantic-sexual dimension of our lives would be likened to a flame that flickers off and on.

As I learned from Michele, it's important for a woman to envision the prize—what sexual fulfillment means to them. Sexuality for my wife and many other women is a part of romance. In the sweaty locker rooms that first introduced me to sexual discussions among men, I heard stories related to sexual exploits and physical mechanics. Sexuality was reduced to a game in which we sought to run bases. As guys, we would often celebrate when our friends said they got to "third base." Although, the question that no one asked was, Where was the concept of romance? Even my father focused on counseling me about what I should *not* do. Fortunately, romantic love can be learned. The challenge for most guys is that they must become sensitized to romance and then learn the unique romantic world of their spouse. It is appropriate to have a dream of how you want to be loved, respected and received in your own marriage. However, the hard part of having a dream is to communicate it and move toward this goal.

Emotional Intimacy

For years, I felt that I hit and missed romantic moments that enhanced both emotional intimacy and sexuality in our relationship. I have sat down to watch many movies with my wife and two daughters. The most challenging for me personally have been the "chick flicks." All three of my girls seem to be so connected as they watch these movies. They'll all sigh at the same time or reach for a tissue together. The classic movie for the women at my house is *Anne of Green Gables*. It's about an orphan who finds friends, fits into a family and ultimately falls in love with Gilbert, a childhood friend. One day, it dawned on me that this movie carried a key to how Michele saw her romantic world. This realization would eventually help me because it allowed me to evaluate my actions and responses to Michele. It gave me a romantic road map that actually enhanced both romance and sexuality in our marriage.

Where do you find a place of emotional intimacy and connection? What does it look like? Is it the *Anne of Green Gables* story, which gives us such a sense of warmth, devotion and attachment? For Anne, three major issues determined how she defined love and acceptance. As an orphan, she had to deal with the fear of abandonment. Then, she needed to have a concrete expression of respect and acceptance from those closest to her. Finally, her friends observed her uniqueness over the years and held her in high esteem. These are all tangible expressions of understanding and trust. Also throughout the story line, her true love singled her out and pursued her. Gilbert understood and celebrated her uniqueness. As I reflected on this movie, I noticed that Michele's life story had more emotional similarities to this story than I ever could have imagined.

Whatever your romantic dream, remember that you won't attain it overnight. Yet you must believe that this kind of relationship is possible if you communicate and work toward it. As task-oriented and high-strung as Michele is, it was hard for me to believe that in her heart of hearts the *Anne of Green Gables* type of relationship was her real goal. Michele was able to help me see the kind of relationship she needed over time.

Verbal Affirmation

A man's muscles and self-reliant exterior do not mean he is equally tough internally. I was easily wounded by the fact that my needs seemed to get pushed aside in the hustle and bustle of our lives. The kids' needs always came first. This is often how men come to feel disrespected. It hurts the husband when a wife tells him, "I am too busy. I don't have time. Please stop." Or if she says, "We can't do this now—I have to cook."

A refusal of sex can be tough for men to handle. If it happens often enough, men begin to feel rejected. Usually they either become sexually aggressive, forcing sex on their wives, or they shut down and stop showing affection. A wounded response of "I'll show her" sometimes leads men into the arms of another woman. When a man begins to feel unattractive to his wife, he starts to wonder whether it is okay for him to make some kind of advance. A man needs verbal affirmation of his attractiveness and that he is meeting his spouse's needs. By affirming your husband, you help yourself. Having sex is not just about a great feeling; it is about giving someone else pleasure. Women, you may need to think, *This expression is for him. I'm going to minister to his needs. I'll make him feel like a hero.*

The apostle Paul tells us, "Do not deprive each other" (1 Cor. 7:5). This means that we are not to deny or withhold sexual intimacy from our spouses. Often men hold back their emotions even as they describe their wives as cold. Sometimes wives hold back their physical bodies and describe their husbands as being only interested in the physical act of sex. When the average woman says "Romance," most guys think, *Sex.* And when guys talk about sex, women include emotion. In summary, our emotional intimacy is part of the joy of sex, and our sexual intimacy can open our heart to deeper emotions.

OVERCOMING TRAUMAS AND WOUNDS

A large percentage of people have had real trauma in their sexual experiences. This is one reason sexual intimacy with your spouse can be an issue of spiritual warfare. Many people have flashbacks of unpleasant experiences during times of lovemaking. Sometimes these images are related to sexual experiences and sometimes not.

Suppressed Feelings

When I was a pastor in upstate New York, a friend named Tom from another church told me that whenever he was moving toward sexual relations with his wife, certain images would pop into his mind. To my surprise, what Tom was dealing with had no sexual context whatsoever. Instead, there was a deep area of shame and bitterness left over from childhood. When Tom was a teenager, a tragedy on the family farm had maimed his brother. Tom had been chopping wood one day and accidentally cut off three fingers from his brother's right hand.

Tom never fully dealt with his feelings of guilt over this situation. He used all sorts of blocking mechanisms to keep his feelings from surfacing, but somehow these strategies stopped working when he became intimate with his wife.

When he let his guard down, his guilt would surface. He was also secretly bitter about how his family and friends had responded to the accident. To help Tom heal, I led him through a process of forgiveness in which he had to identify the presence of these old hurts and release them to the Lord. This began a healing process in several aspects of his life, including sexual intimacy.

Painful Memories

Bitterness often opens the door for mental harassment. Many of us are vulnerable to memories stemming from unresolved internal conflict. If guilt and anger unrelated to sexuality can cause us problems like it did for my friend, imagine if your bitterness is directly related to sexual trauma (such as rape or sexual abuse). When a woman is in an intimate situation, her husband's tone of voice or certain words might trigger painful memories. The way to become free from this harassment is by releasing the person who hurt you and forgiving them. This kind of forgiveness may require personal counseling to achieve.

The writer of Hebrews tell us:

See to it that no one misses the grace of God and that no bitter root grows up to cause trouble and defile many. See that no one is sexually immoral, or is godless like Esau, who for a single meal sold his inheritance rights as the oldest son (12:15-16).

The root of bitterness yields many different kinds of problems—mental harassment is just one of them. Do you have unresolved issues with people, such as bitterness, guilt or regret? If we do not embrace God's grace, we can easily fall prey to a root of bitterness and the negative fruit it produces.

CORRECTING MYTHS

People in our society have many myths and misconceptions about sex, and I could fill the rest of this book addressing them. But I will briefly discuss two of the most common myths.

Everyone Else Is Sexually Satisfied

If average Americans were experiencing great sex in their own bedrooms, they would not be so fascinated with the ideas and images beyond their own marriages. Outside sexual experiences, whether real or imagined, never enhance marital sex. Like children eating nonnutritious snacks between meals, the sexual practices of many Americans take away their appetite for the healthy and normal sex life. Some reports indicate that 20 percent of marriages are impacted by the adultery of one of the spouses—and this is a conservative estimate.[5]

If you are engaging in any activity that undermines sexual satisfaction in marriage, it's time to ask for God's help and your spouse's understanding. Is the problem physiological, spiritual, emotional or habitual? As you confront your issue, you may need to seek help from a counselor or pastor.

Two issues frequently diminish sexual fulfillment: sexual addictions and childhood abuse. Addictions can grow to the point where people prefer to fantasize about adulterous sex than actually to have sex with their spouse. The fact that the viewing public clamors for sex in movies only confirms that people would rather enjoy a vicarious thrill than deal with their relationship issues that hinder great sex at home.

In regard to childhood traumas, it is estimated that more than one-third of all women have been sexually abused. A growing number of men have also become the victims of incest or molestation. Both men and women bring these painful experiences into marriage. Many people need a restoration of sexual innocence and healing from past traumas. This is accomplished through the power of Christ and can be facilitated in the context of a loving marriage. Open communication about our mutual needs will create an atmosphere in which healing and cleansing can occur.

I'm the Only One Experiencing Problems
There is a combination of myth, folklore and miscommunication surrounding male and female sexual performance. Secret fears of inadequacy and unattractiveness plague many men and women. Marriage partners need to see the importance of creating godly mental habits with regard to sexual fulfillment. After counseling many couples, my perception is that 95 percent of sexual activity is based on the thought life and imagination, and only 5 percent is based on the physical.

Our imagination can be stamped with romantic concepts of sex or defiled by dirty stories, myths and pain. Our history and thought lives affect our present activity. Also, demonic influences can entrap us in prisons of unfulfillment. Therefore, we must seize control of our most intimate equipment—our minds. Both men and women are experiencing an incredible satanic assault on their self-esteem because of society's unrealistic emphasis on sex.

FREQUENTLY ASKED QUESTIONS

As I have counseled people on problems related to sexuality, several issues and questions have repeatedly surfaced. These questions are addressed below, and I will begin each answer with a pertinent Scripture passage.

What Is Sexual Purity?

I made a covenant with my eyes not to look lustfully at a girl. For what is man's lot from God above, his heritage from the Almighty on high? Is it not ruin for the wicked, disaster for those who do wrong? Does he not see my ways and count my every step? (Job 31:1-4).

When Christian singles ask me about purity, it is often in regard to specific acts and behaviors. They want to know at what point they cross the line into sinfulness. Other times, men will ask me, usually in hushed tones, "Do you think *this* act or *that* act is okay for a Christian?" My answer is always that sexual purity begins in the *heart* and *mind*.

Based on James 1:13-17, any sinful act is the result of a four-step process:

1. thought;
2. affection or lust;
3. decision;
4. action.

If I keep my thoughts in check, I have remained pure. I have been tempted but *not* tarnished. Unfortunately, it's possible to burn with lust long before I commit the act. This does not mean that I can't have sexual thoughts I simply don't want to dwell on the wrong acts with the wrong people. Sexual purity starts in the mind, which directs our actions. We want to make sure that we keep our thought life centered on God.

Can a Husband or Wife Be Friends with Someone of the Opposite Sex Outside of Their Marriage?

Then the LORD God made a woman from the rib he had taken out of the man, and he brought her to the man. The man said, "This is now bone of my bones and flesh of my flesh; she shall be called 'woman,' for she was taken out of man." For this reason a man will leave his father and mother and be united to his wife, and they will become one flesh. The man and his wife were both naked, and they felt no shame. (Gen. 2:22-25)

I believe it is okay for members of the opposite sex to be friends, so long as careful boundaries are adhered to. I can have friendships with women at church and in my community. However, there is a level of emotional intimacy that I reserve only for my spouse. When the verse above says that the man and woman "felt no shame," the focus is on emotional vulnerability symbolized by physical nakedness. Therefore, I must be extremely cautious to preserve this kind of emotional openness only for my spouse. I must not fall into *emotional* adultery with a woman, which will likely lead to *physical* infidelity.

Additionally, as a man, I cannot discuss my marital problems with another woman. I also refuse to tell or listen to off-color jokes with a member of the opposite sex. Years ago Billy Graham and the other leaders of Youth for Christ made a vow not to ride in a car or elevator with a woman alone. This was to protect themselves against perceived wrongdoing and emotional adultery that can lead to other things.

It's important to note that affairs most often begin with an emotional connection—often an innocent friendship that becomes too close and too intense. If you do not trust yourself to maintain clear boundaries in opposite-sex friendships, then it's best to avoid them altogether.

Is It Okay to Withhold Sex from Your Mate?

The husband should fulfill his marital duty to his wife, and likewise the wife to her husband. The wife's body does not belong to her alone but also to her husband. In the same way, the husband's body does not belong to him alone but also to his wife. Do not deprive each other except by mutual consent. . . . Then come together again so that Satan will not tempt you because of your lack of self-control (1 Cor. 7:3-5).

This passage is clear enough—you should not withhold sex from your spouse. Often, when men or women withhold sex from their spouses, there is unresolved anger or lingering resentment. These issues should be taken care of so spouses can enjoy a healthy, loving sex life.

Sometimes women use sex as a "bargaining chip" to get their husbands to agree to something they want. This is nothing more than a manipulative power play that establishes a destructive pay-me-for-my-favors arrangement. Other women may feel justified in sternly sending their husbands to the couch as a disciplinary action. Ploys such as these bring great trauma to the emotional intimacy of a couple's union. We must remember that sex in marriage is based on a prenegotiated covenant, and any kind of manipulation undermines that sacred vow.

Of course, men can be just as coercive when it comes to sex. There are two kinds of men who delight in demanding sex from their spouse. The first is a man I call Leon the Lecturer. He will rationalize that there is nothing wrong with him, yet he will lecture his wife or rub her nose in the fact that it's her *duty* to serve him. The second kind of man is David the Demander. He often feels disrespected by his spouse, so he demands his conjugal rights. Many women will feel justified to tell this type of husband, "Sorry, no sex tonight!" Unfortunately, a wife will only cause the problem to worsen by saying no. This would be tantamount to pouring salt into an open wound. When a man feels rebuffed and rejected, he may respond in fits of anger or emotional withdrawal.

Is Masturbation in Marriage Okay?

> For this reason a man will leave his father and mother and be united to his wife, and they will become one flesh (Gen. 2:24).

Men are often rightly accused of forgetting affection and touch aside from the pleasure of sex. So when a man masturbates, he further denies his wife physical warmth and tenderness. Moreover, this practice may allow a man to avoid confronting problems that have emerged in his marital sex life. He may achieve sexual release while ignoring relational issues that should be addressed.

Female masturbation also breaks the intimacy cycle. Further, it can create the kind of intense pleasure with which few men can compete. Specialized sexual equipment for women seems to be selling at an alarming rate. Therefore, the imaginary lover can outperform one's husband. Does this strengthen a couple's sex life or weaken it? The answer is obvious.

What Do I Do If My Mate Is Unable to Have Sex?

> Husbands, in the same way be considerate as you live with your wives, and treat them with respect as the weaker partner and as heirs with you of the gracious gift of life (1 Pet. 3:7).

> Train the younger women to love their husbands (Titus 2:4).

The basis for every aspect of marriage—including sexuality—is love, respect and honor. Therefore, if a husband or wife is unable to perform sexually because of a physical problem or unresolved emotional trauma, the partner should respond gently and lovingly. It would do absolutely no good to turn up the pressure on the spouse who cannot engage in sex for whatever reason.

What is more, I believe that any kind of sexual dysfunction or difficulty must remain confidential. Men, whose virility has been measured in terms of sexual prowess, will feel ashamed if others know about his problem. First Corinthians 3:7 declares that it is the husband's responsibility to meet the needs of his wife. Men suffering from impotency or a temporary decline of sexual interest may need to be coached by their spouse. By sensitively sharing her needs, the wife may guide him toward giving affection and sexual gratification.

> The basis for every aspect of marriage— including sexuality— is love, respect and honor.

The author of the classic book *Intended for Pleasure* makes this emphatic statement:

> Impotence is not a natural development of old age but is almost always a result of the state of mind at any age, affecting the man who worries about the normal changes taking place in his body or who sees himself as "over the hill." Although diabetes creates an inability to develop a full erection in 50 percent of men, only about 2 to 3 percent of men suffering from this malady are unable to be brought to the point of sexual release.[6]

Women who are unable to reach climax are less likely to feel the same level of social embarrassment as men. However, I don't want to minimize the sense of loss that a hysterectomy or other medical procedures can have on the emotional makeup of a woman. Dr. Ed Wheat insists that it is important to talk about fears of sexual loss prior to surgery with both the husband and wife. He says that in his experience, "the only change may be an improvement in their sex life."[7]

There must be sensitive communication about our needs. Additionally, we as couples need to recognize that emotional intimacy is our goal. It is a God-given privilege to minister to each other's needs. Spouses are not required to be perfect, but they are expected to be responsive in an attitude of love and honor.

Should I Tell My Mate About Past Affairs?

Confess your sins to each other and pray for each other so that you may be healed (Jas. 5:16).

The spirit of this verse is that, generally, we as Christians should acknowledge our shortcomings and failures to brothers and sisters in the faith. The old adage is right: Confession is good for the soul. But does this mean we should, in every instance, divulge our sins and misdeeds to our partner? I believe we need to be honest and open with our spouses, as any kind of secret erodes trust and intimacy. However, when it comes to past relationships or affairs, you do not need to go into detail and tell *everything*.

My youngest daughter, Elizabeth, has an expression: "That's T.M.I." This stands for Too Much Information. Although openness is good, vivid details about your sexual history may be damaging. How many serious girlfriends did you have? is a fair question. However, a detailed description of each relationship may be T.M.I.

Dr. Willard Harley has helped me immensely in understanding the nuances of honest communication. He says that there are five parts to being totally open with your spouse. These five parts are: emotional honesty, historical honesty, current honesty, future honesty and complete honesty.[8] It seems to me that historical honesty is important, but we may want to avoid graphic details that could wound or offend.

As a pastor, I have had to bury several people who were HIV positive. Obviously, spouses need to know about sexually transmitted diseases or other information that will affect them. Newlyweds and courting couples may well need more specific details than I would have deemed necessary in the past. And in the interest of maintaining trust in the relationship, let your spouse hear potential problems up front from you instead of through the rumor mill.

My Spouse Wants Oral Sex. Do I Have to Submit to This?

Marriage should be honored by all, and the marriage bed kept pure (Heb. 13:4).

The Bible seems to be silent on the specifics of oral sex; therefore, we must reach for an overarching principle. Demanding this kind of physical expression is troublesome to me. In marriage, it's fair for both parties to negotiate the style and variety of emotional and physical intimacy. Honor and respect for our mates dictate that we should not pressure them to do anything they are uncomfortable with.

Married couples should talk about how exotic sexual practices make them feel. If something makes you feel unclean or violated, you must let your spouse know. Your conscience and sensitivities must be honored.

CONCLUSION

This chapter has covered a wide range of topics, yet there has been one theme running throughout the pages—sex the way

God intended is awesome! His goal has always been to fulfill emotional intimacy between husband and wife. This intimacy is only achieved and maintained by couples who learn to talk openly with each other about their needs and who courageously confront issues that thwart sexual satisfaction. Spouses must exercise nonjudgmental, unconditional love in order to maximize sexual love.

To make your marriage as great as it can be, you must approach sex as a prize worth pursuing and then make the effort necessary to attain the prize. Make this aspect of your relationship a source of joy and delight. That's exactly what God intended!

CHAPTER 9

MONEY MATTERS

Making Sense of Your Dollars and Cents

I never lose an opportunity of urging a practical beginning, however small, for it is wonderful how often the mustard seed germinates and roots itself.

Florence Nightingale

Forty years after Napoleon retreated from Russia—losing 90 percent of the largest standing army in history—an ambitious tsar aimed to take control of the Balkans of Eastern Europe. On November 30, 1853, the Russian navy defeated a weak Turkish squadron in a place called Sinop.

Knowing that Napoleon's largest fighting force couldn't conquer Russia, the British and French formed an alliance. They used new weapons to strike an old enemy and started a war over the Ottoman Empire. These enemies-turned-allies were determined to keep the Russian fleet out of the Eastern Mediterranean. The British-French alliance had one objective—to destroy or capture the nerve center of Russia's naval power, the dockyard at Sebastopol in Crimea (modern-day Ukraine).

During the height of the war, the Russians were losing 1,000 men a day because of the allies' new, more powerful weaponry. Despite the fierce fighting, most of the soldiers who died lost their lives not to artillery fire but to disease. Many of the injured were taken to hospitals plagued with unsanitary conditions.

Out of this bleak backdrop emerged an unlikely heroine, a young Christian nurse named Florence Nightingale. Born in 1820 in Florence, Italy, to a wealthy family, Nightingale was raised mostly in Darbyshire, England. She learned five languages and was taught to read the Bible from the Greek text by her banker father. At age 17, Florence gave her life to God's specific plan.

Soon Nightingale became instrumental in cleaning up the deplorable hospital conditions that claimed so many lives in Crimea. Using her intense compassion coupled with her intellect, Florence Nightingale raised the efficiency and status of nurses in the nineteenth century. In 1860, she founded the Nightingale School for Nurses, which was the first school of its kind in the world.

Nightingale went on to be a leading figure in the reform of medical treatment and, even today, her name is widely recognized and associated with compassionate, dedicated care. She soon became a woman acting on a clear, personal vision. She had no idea when she first left England that she would turn the tide of both medicine and the Crimean war.[1]

The story of Florence Nightingale gives encouragement to a common problem occurring in many homes—the discord and dissension over finances and money management. Family finances often serve as a battleground, but out of this conflict can come heroic efforts. Victory can be secured despite overwhelming odds, and long-term improvements can result from short-term sacrifice. Using Nightingale as our model, many of us need to use both our *heart* and our *mind* to address our financial difficulties strategically. We can clean up our monetary mess and look forward to a healthy, happy future.

LESSONS LEARNED

Like most families, ours has endured its share of financial ups and downs, successes and setbacks. Many times we've squabbled over money; other times we've rejoiced together at God's provision. Here's a glimpse into our financial history from Michele's perspective.

When we first married, everything we purchased was second- or thirdhand and in continual disrepair. Some appliance or another was always on the fritz. If the washing machine happened to be working, then the vacuum would quit. If the coffeepot percolated, then the toaster would go on strike. One of the lamps responded to the "on" switch only when it got good and ready. Conversely, the Crock-Pot was always on and assisted in many burnt offerings served at dinner.

Using broken appliances week in and week out had me at the boiling point (especially when our stove wouldn't bring anything to a boil). I was not only upset that they didn't work, but also that there was no money to replace them. Worst of all, Harry was unable to fix them. I dreamt of Harry handing me the faulty appliance in working order or surprising me with a brand-new replacement. Nevertheless, he returned daily from the office with only his briefcase, Stetson and overcoat.

I remember screaming at the top of my lungs about the microwave oven that went on the blink again. Harry's response? He proceeded to pray. In the midst of my cynicism, Harry was calm and confident. At the end of his prayer, the microwave began to work and has been working ever since! Three things truly amazed me that day.

1. The level of frustration I allowed to develop over something I couldn't change.
2. Harry's confidence in God to hear and answer when he prayed about anything.
3. The fact that the microwave continues to work 15 years later.

Michele's perspective on the spiritual dynamic that belies our financial breakthroughs is important. James 2:17 says that faith without works is dead. The way we handle our finances is not just a matter of economics—it's a *faith* issue. In the following pages, I want to present some ideas about money that will promote harmony in your family and honor God in the process. Specifically, I want to address your philosophy of finances, your strategy of money management and how to get out of a tough situation.

ECONOMIC PHILOSOPHIES

Everyone has a philosophy about personal finance, but many people never stop to think about how they use (or abuse) their money. I believe three areas most influence our philosophy of finance.

1. *Our heritage.* This includes our background or roots. Whether we grow up rich or poor or somewhere in between greatly affects our views toward money.
2. *Our worldview.* For instance, if you are a Christian, you probably believe money is something to be shared and used to expand God's kingdom. On the other hand, non-Christians might view money as something to be hoarded and used to enrich themselves and their families.
3. *Our personal problems.* People who lack self-control may spend more than they should. People who don't trust God to provide may save obsessively as a hedge against disaster.

Our Heritage

When I was growing up my father would jokingly say that my mother would travel all the way across town to save 10 cents on a loaf of bread. It was always funny to him how Mom would clip coupons and organize her shopping to take advantage of a sale. She would even plan for Christmas purchases six to eight months ahead of time. Because she was extremely frugal, she always got great deals.

Of course, my Dad had his own unique spending habits. He always stayed within his budget, but he tended to buy flashy and frivolous items. Dad would eat at the neighborhood greasy spoon to save a buck, but then he'd make some extravagant purchase elsewhere. I remember the day he bought himself a beautiful diamond ring. Because we lived in a crime-filled community, when people observed his ring, he would sometimes laughingly say, "It's amazing what they can do with zirconium these days."

I often thought to myself, *Why would you buy a ring that you'd have to hide from people in your neighborhood? Did it mean that much to you?* Obviously it did to this son of a mulatto housekeeper (Evell

Keith) and a South Carolinian of West Indian decent (Simmie Jackson). The ring was more than a piece of jewelry to Dad; it was a symbol of achievement. It was more valuable on the troubled streets of Avondale in Cincinnati, Ohio, than the first college degree of the Jackson family that adorned his walls at home.

> Conflict often arises because spouses are merging two completely different viewpoints about money.

With these two pieces of information alone, you have a hint about my own perspective toward money. I tend to be frugal in some aspects, and then turn around and buy a high-fashion item. This may be why I drive a 10-year-old Mercedes Benz that looks like new, but still travel across town to catch a good deal.

How does your heritage influence your financial perspective? How about your spouse's background? Conflict often arises because spouses are merging two completely different viewpoints about money. When settling on an approach to your family's spending, perhaps you can compromise to allow for each spouse's family idiosyncrasies.

Our Worldview

Michele and I developed a scriptural foundation for financial stewardship. Before we had rededicated our lives to the Lord, our goal was to get rich, rich, rich. But being committed to the principles of God's economy radically changed our thinking. The Scriptures caused us to reevaluate our ambitions. Here are a few of our favorite passages on this subject.

> Do not store up for yourselves treasures on earth, where moth and rust destroy, and where thieves break in and

steal. But store up for yourselves treasures in heaven, where moth and rust do not destroy, and where thieves do not break in and steal. For where your treasure is, there your heart will be also (Matt. 6:19-21).

No one can serve two masters. . . . You cannot serve both God and Money (Matt. 6:24).

Be shepherds of God's flock that is under your care . . . not greedy for money, but eager to serve (1 Pet. 5:2).

We acknowledge that God owns everything, and we are merely trustees of whatever He lends us. Therefore, we have chosen to give a sizeable portion of our income to the church and mission outreaches. God has answered many of our prayers regarding finances and possessions (including the microwave oven Michele mentioned) because of our covenant with Him about money.

In addition to my Christian faith, the generation in which I grew up has also shaped my worldview. For example, Baby Boomers (which includes me) generally want everything now and are not afraid to leverage their future to get it. The ability to delay gratification is not a characteristic value of this generation. Conversely, the Builder generation of World War II went through the Great Depression; therefore, they are much more security oriented and usually want to pay cash for everything. There's little doubt that cultural and generational influences greatly impact our individual perspectives about money.

Our Personal Problems
Our personal problems definitely affect our money management and spending habits. For you, it may be impulse purchases of

sweets that can add up to $600 a year. Perhaps you struggle with selfishness, which keeps you from tithing and giving as much as you should. It could be that financial equality is an issue—you spend freely while harping on your spouse for every little purchase.

Every couple needs to sit down and work through the ideas that they have about finance. Although their individual philosophies might cause them to clash, they need to communicate and come up with a coherent, consistent philosophy. Then after the philosophy is set, the couple can tackle the big questions of family finance. When should they use debt? When and how do they want to buy a house? How much will they save for retirement? Sometimes one or both spouses' beliefs will not be in sync with God's perspective on money. The Bible's instructions about how we are to handle finances are quite clear. The key is for both husband and wife to be receptive and responsive to the Lord's leading. I believe that as couples study God's Word and follow His financial advice, many conflicts will work themselves out.

Now let me bring these thoughts home by asking you a few specific questions.

- How would you describe your philosophy of finance? Be as specific as possible.
- How did your family upbringing and cultural influence shape your views toward money?
- How have the differences in your background and your spouse's background created conflict around money management?
- If you were going to write a mission statement regarding the use of your finances, what would it be?

STRATEGIC PLANNING

In chapter 4, I talked about creating a strategy for your family destiny. If you apply those principles and decide on specific family goals, it will be easier (which isn't to say *easy*) to allocate your financial resources accordingly. A clear-cut strategy will help you decide on the things to which you should say yes and, perhaps more importantly, those to which you should say no.

When I talk about strategy, I simply mean that you determine a long-term destination and lay out the steps to get there. Many people move through the child-rearing years or toward retirement without identifying their goals. They go on impulses and whims without following God's master plan. Strategy has, at its root, an understanding of the big picture as well as each season of life.

For example, a budget is just a strategic tool designed to help you meet your goals. During this time of financial planning, remember that you don't serve a budget; it is meant to serve you. Financial expert Larry Burkett has a helpful guide for developing a budget. As he walks you through a line-by-line process, he provides percentages for how the average family allocates its resources.[2] I have included a sample budget, which you can use as a guideline for your own plan. You will need to adjust the percentages to facilitate your family's long-term strategy, which will allow you to reach the destiny God has ordained for you.

PERCENTAGE GUIDE FOR FAMILY INCOME

Gross Income	15,000	20,000	40,000	50,000	60,000
Tithe	10%	10%	10%	10%	10%
Taxes	12%	14%	15%	17%	21%
Net Spendables	11,700	15,200	30,000	36,500	41,400
Housing	32%	30%	28%	25%	25%
Auto	15%	15%	12%	12%	12%
Food	15%	16%	14%	14%	10%
Insurance	5%	5%	5%	5%	5%
Entertainment/ Recreation	7%	7%	7%	7%	7%
Clothing	5%	5%	5%	6%	6%

Medical/Dental	5%	5%	4%	4%	4%
Miscellaneous	6%	7%	7%	8%	8%
Savings	5%	5%	5%	5%	5%
Debts	5%	5%	5%	5%	5%
Investments	—	—	8%	9%	13%

STRATEGIC SAVING

In order to reach my family's long-term financial strategy, my rule of thumb is that I put my money into at least three basic pots.

Long-Term Savings
I have a long-term savings pot. Unlike my budget, I want my savings goals to be absolute numbers instead of percentages. It is important for my long-term savings to serve a specific and meaningful purpose such as retirement, my kids' college education or a dream vacation for my wife and me. The less specific I am about my long-term goals, the harder it is to comply with them consistently.

Short-Term Savings
I need a short-term savings pot. This is available cash that I can get my hands on if I need short-term emergency funds. If the air-conditioning goes out or the car needs repairs, I have a source of money. If my short-term savings goal is $3,000, I will push myself to accumulate this amount. Further, if I have occasion to use this fund, replacement of the money is also a high priority.

Checking Account
The third pot is the day-to-day cash flow. From this pot I must finance ongoing expenses and have enough money left over to put something in my short-term emergency pot and my long-term savings. Most of us intuitively understand that we cannot

spend more money than we take in. Unfortunately, we mask this reality by going into debt.

Consider a few key questions to help you think through your specific situation.

- How does your financial management (budgeting, saving and so on) either facilitate or foil your long-range family strategy?
- In what ways is your financial strategy part of your Strategy for Family Destiny? (See chapter 4 for a refresher on this concept.)
- Which budget item might give you the most trouble? How can you correct this?
- What is your number one financial goal for the coming year? The next five years?

A TURNAROUND PRESCRIPTION

The common saying "Expect the unexpected" is certainly true in the area of family finances. Once something catastrophic happens, it seems to throw philosophy and strategy out the window.

Think for a moment about the soldiers under the care of Florence Nightingale and her dedicated band of nurses. I imagine that each of those soldiers had a radical change of perspective once they were injured. Their thoughts shifted from *Will I help our army achieve victory?* to *Will I live?* The goal for every injured soldier becomes clear and simple—get well. This is the same issue couples and families must address when they encounter financial hardship: How can we overcome our current crisis and get well?

I have frequently talked to people in crisis who have said, "I just don't know what I am going to do." Two months later they are still in that same place, but with one major exception—their debt has increased.

As with patients in a hospital, people with money problems need a treatment plan. At the beginning of this chapter, I quoted Florence Nightingale, who once said, "We must take practical steps now to make a difference."[3] With this in mind, I offer the following prescriptions for turning around a bad financial situation.

Rx #1: Stop the Bleeding

Find out exactly what is draining your cash or racking up debts. Decide which expenses you can cut immediately. What are some ways you can save big chunks of money? Move to a less-expensive apartment. Sell your luxury car and buy a cheap economy model. Then move on to smaller purchases. What are some ways you can save little chunks of money (which have a way of adding up)? Cancel your cable TV subscription. Start carpooling to work. Skip the daily latte.

Stopping the bleeding may involve creative restructuring of your expenses. If you have recently gone through a divorce or you are under threat of bankruptcy or repossession, you may have to take drastic restructuring measures. Most people in these situations are guilty of attempting to do too much too late. They get behind in one or two important payments and wind up robbing Peter to pay Paul. That is to say, they take a payment that is actually late for the car and put it toward their mortgage account to avoid penalties.

It is possible that an unforeseen crisis will occur and the whole house of cards will fall apart. In order to avoid this scenario, you may have to build up a substantial emergency fund (short-term savings). Think of it as building a much-needed war chest. One way to build a large war chest is to decide how much money you need to reach a comfortable financial goal. Next, admit that you are in a crisis and that you are going to take action. You may want to negotiate lower terms for outstanding bills right away.

Proactive communication will buy you time; many creditors will extend mercy to a conscientious person who makes commitments and follows through. If you wait until the creditors call, you will feel like a heel and they will think you're a deadbeat. In extreme cases, it may be necessary to engage an accountant or an attorney to help you walk through this challenging process.

Rx #2: Hook Up an IV

Patients are often connected to intravenous machines that release consistent doses of medicine and replenish nutrients. Think about what can give you an immediate though temporary infusion of cash. Can you moonlight to generate extra income? Can you sell off your exercise equipment that's gathering dust in the garage? Your immediate goal is to get cash flowing *in* rather than *out*.

Rx #3: Consult a Specialist

Many excellent books, websites and other resources are available from top-notch financial experts. These can provide far more detailed information than I can offer in the space of one chapter. You may need specific guidance on debt reduction, paying back taxes and whether or not to file for bankruptcy. Many helpful books are on the market written from a Christian perspective.[4] In some cases, you may need to meet with a financial advisor face-to-face.

Rx #4: Begin Rehabilitation

Once you have dealt with the immediate crisis and sought advice from experts, you can devise a longer-term plan to cure your financial ills. You take your medicine, go through a therapy regimen and strengthen yourself to regain full health. This means you come up with a plan to pay off debts, seek ways to increase your income and replenish a depleted savings account. Does all of this happen quickly or easily? Absolutely not! Rehabilitation sometimes takes years and can be painful at times. But you must work diligently to achieve your goal, and steadily your financial state will strengthen.

Rx #5: Plan for Full Recovery

In chapter 4, I told you about when I reached age 40, was diagnosed as prediabetic and found myself considerably overweight. I did not need a quick fix but a lifestyle change! This included a change in diet and the start of a consistent exercise regimen, which continues to this day. People who have encountered financial setbacks also need a lifestyle adjustment to ensure their continual health. They must correct bad habits that have developed over time so they don't relapse into financial burdens.

Those in tough circumstances need to learn sound financial principles and develop personal discipline so they can live within their means. If accumulating debt is a continual problem, they need to put aside money in a short-term savings pot so they won't have to rely on credit cards when surprise expenses show up. Long-term financial health is not possible without this bottom-line attention to debt.

FREQUENTLY ASKED QUESTIONS

I want to close out this discussion by answering six of the most frequently asked financial questions that I hear.

I Pray to God for Help with My Finances, but I Still Always Have Money Problems. Is God Hearing Me?

First of all, if you are praying with a sincere and humble heart, you can be absolutely positive God is listening to you. God has His own reasons for answering your prayers in His time. Begin by making sure that you are being obedient to God's instructions regarding money (and all of His instructions for that matter). I suggest you do a careful study on all the verses related to money, giving, tithing, wealth, debt and so on. Then apply those lessons to your own situation. You'll be surprised how much clear-cut direction as well as general principles the Bible has to offer.

Next, it's important to follow Florence Nightingale's approach of using the mind and the heart together. For Christians that means having faith in God to meet our needs *and* using the smarts He gave us to handle our money wisely. I am amazed at how many believers expect God to rescue them out of financial problems, and yet they never take steps to seek help. God can certainly supply all your needs and you must trust Him, but He also wants you to use the intellect and common sense He gave you.

My Spouse and I Always Fight About Money. What Should We Do?

Go back and review the earlier discussions in this book on communication and conflict resolution (chapters 5 and 6). Apply the information from those chapters to your financial disagreements. The principles of healthy, productive communication apply to all aspects of marriage, including the use of money.

I also suggest that you and your spouse read this finance chapter together. So many marital conflicts about money stem from our background and upbringing. We fail to understand the differing expectations and habits we carry into marriage. Simply realizing where your partner is coming from and communicating your own background helps avoid many arguments. Talking about spending habits in advance will alleviate unpleasant surprises later. Be sure to discuss what you believe the Bible is telling you to do with your finances, and take the whole issue to the Lord in prayer.

Next, you and your spouse need to agree on your family strategy. When you decide your long-range plans together, many financial questions will answer themselves. For instance, if paying for your children's college education is a high priority, then you will need to set aside a significant portion of your family income to reach this goal. If you dream of going on a summer-long mission trip as a family, you'll need to sacrifice in some areas to make this happen.

How Can I Prepare for My Children's College Education?
Three questions are important for parents to consider.

1. What percentage of our child's undergraduate education or trade school will we fund?
2. Is it important that our child attend a top-notch school or will a solid-but-unprestigious one do?
3. What way will we use debt to finance our child's education?

There are no right or wrong answers to these questions, so I'll give an example of the approach Michele and I took. We decided we would pay for all the undergraduate education for our daughters, but they would be responsible for anything beyond their bachelor's degree. Next, we believe that low-interest loans make borrowing for school a great option. Therefore, we started a savings program with the understanding that we could make up the difference through loans we would pay off over a 20-year period. These kinds of loans can be tied to home equity and are not very expensive on a monthly basis. Finally, if our daughters were accepted at a prestigious institution, we would send them to the best school.

If you're planning to borrow money, you'll still have to understand your personal debt capacity. Start saving money as early as possible and apply for loans five years before your child begins college. Try downloading applications from the Internet, and then get a qualified consultant to help you fill out appropriate applications and plan accordingly. The analysis that you have to make is whether you should pay your child's tuition up front (if possible) or let your savings earn the maximum interest in the investment vehicles you have. However you decide to fund your child's education, let me encourage you to think big and take long-term action. Give your child the best you can.

Our Family Doesn't Communicate Well About Finances, Which Causes Many Problems. What Can We Do?

Start by holding a "state of the union" meeting each month (either with the entire family or just the spouses—whichever is appropriate). Here you review your short-term and long-term goals to make sure you're moving toward them; address any concerns or questions; and review your budget to see if you're sticking to it. This is also a time when you can discuss all the nitty-gritty financial issues such as, "Did you call the utility company to check on our last bill? What did you think of the estimate for the roof repair?"

Once you get your finances in order and establish a routine, the meeting can be shortened from, say, a half hour to 10 minutes. At this point in our lives, Michele and I work toward the big picture. Since she manages the monthly bills, I only want to know whether or not we are on track to meet our goals. Therefore, unless we're discussing a major purchase or big decision, our meetings are more like five-minute checkups than thorough diagnostic examinations.

I'm Thinking of Quitting My Job to Start My Own Business. Should I?

Obviously, I can't go into much detail here, but let me give you a few general principles to consider. You have to decide whether you are going to start a home-based business or a major venture. Both types of businesses have unique advantages, but they must each be considered carefully. A home business may be making clothes, multilevel marketing, personal training or a myriad of other endeavors that usually require less time and produce a short sales-to-profit cycle. In other words, you get paid proportionate to your investment of time in a relatively quick fashion. There are no large inventories, and there are no large sums of money that must be floated for a long period of time.

A major venture requires a large business plan, a lot of forethought and an assessment of personal skills. It also demands technical skills, leased office space and equipment. Part of the success of the business will depend on the fitting personality and skills of the entrepreneur. I have been amazed at how many people have decided to start a business that required them to sell a product or service, yet they didn't have the temperament or training to be an effective salesperson. They were simply captivated by the allure of "being my own boss." Think long and hard about what you will be doing day in and day out. Choose a business you are passionate about. If you can't stand rejection, sales is not for you. If the thought of sitting in front of a computer all day makes you stir-crazy, don't start a desktop publishing business.

Many new businesses fail because the proprietor had unrealistic expectations. I've met a lot of people who chomped at the bit to get out of a boring job, so they launched a business without realistically asking, Can this really replace my current salary plus benefits? Wanting to escape one bad situation, they inadvertently create another one. Before beginning a new business, ask yourself, What is the money-making premise of my business? and What are the risk factors of my business? My grandfather was an excellent small businessman who had a rule that is worth considering: Never invest money in a business that you can't afford to lose.

How Do I Find a Good, Reliable Financial Advisor?

Here are some questions to ask potential advisors:

1. What are your credentials and qualifications? Where did you receive your license? Do you belong to any professional organizations?
2. How long have you practiced in the field of finance? May I see references of clients you have served?
3. What is your process for monitoring my goals? Do you sell or use specific products? What are your fees?

Discernment is the key. The reason to use financial advisors is to help guide you in ways that will facilitate your family's goals. Many people confuse the term advisor with broker or salesman. There are some financial advisors who specialize in debt consolidation, personal business turnaround or restructuring clients' credit. There are other financial advisors, typically known as brokers, who represent major companies and sell a myriad of products. Occasionally, the salesmen present themselves as consultants or advisors. A true advisor would require a consulting fee or some kind of remuneration. Once you understand the person's business motivation, you will understand how heavily to weigh his or her advice.

TYPES OF FINANCIAL ADVISORS

Barbara Loos in *I Haven't Saved a Dime, Now What?!* provides a general overview of four different types of financial advisors and their expertise in the marketplace.[5]

Advisor	Expertise
CPA: Certified Public Accountant	Qualified to do high-level accounting and taxes through a rigorous testing process.
CFP: Certified Financial Planner	Qualified through tests to advise on a wide range of financial areas, from taxes to insurance.
CFA: Certified Financial Analyst	Qualified to advise on investments due to passing a series of in-depth tests.
CLU: Chartered Life Underwriter	Qualified to advise on life insurance planning through a test they have passed.

ON LOAN FROM GOD

Underlying all of the principles in this chapter is the fact that God owns everything, yet He lends us money so we can accomplish something great with it. We can use the resources He gives us to advance His kingdom and fulfill the destiny to which He calls our families. The investments we make can pay eternal dividends. The most important question regarding your finances is: How are we going to use the money God gives us to glorify Him?

Like Florence Nightingale who cleaned up the unsanitary conditions in wartime hospitals, we can use our minds and hearts to change the future for our families. You can make changes today that will greatly affect your future.

God never intended money to be a source of conflict for couples. He desires that we use the resources He gives us—however much or little—to enable our families to fulfill a unique calling. Let's rededicate ourselves to following the Lord's economic stimulus plan.

CHAPTER 10

IN-LAWS AND OUTLAWS

Civil Wars

I detest the term "friendly fire." Once a bullet leaves a muzzle or a rocket leaves an airplane, it is not friendly to anyone. Unfortunately, fratricide has been around since the beginning of war. The very chaotic nature of the battlefield, where quick decisions make the difference between life and death, has resulted in numerous incidents of troops being killed by their own fire.

General H. Norman Schwarzkopf, *It Doesn't Take a Hero*

During the winter of 1863, Ulysses S. Grant's Vicksburg campaign was at a standstill. The Union army, bogged down by incessant rains and high waters, faced the possibility of staying put until March or later. The army would be idle for a long time. And when troops are idle, problems seem to emerge as soldiers invent wild ways to distract themselves from boredom and stress.

One day, Mary Livermore, who headed a delegation from the sanitation commission, visited Grant's headquarters. She had learned of 21 seriously ill soldiers who needed to be discharged and sent home to convalesce or risked death. However, the appropriate paperwork had somehow been misplaced, so the men couldn't leave. The matter was pushed up through the ranks, one layer of authority after another, without anyone supplying the proper paperwork or taking responsibility.

Finally, Ms. Livermore located the discharge papers and brought them directly to Grant, who was busily planning the next military campaign. As she talked to the general, he mumbled that there wasn't much he could do about it. But the next day, Grant broke all the rules of protocol and standard operating procedures by discharging these men because he was concerned for their health.

During this time, there was a great deal of rumormongering, infighting and gossiping that rose among the troops as they continued to wait through the winter. Grant himself said this in his memoirs:

> This long, dreary . . . unprecedented winter was one of great hardship to all engaged about Vicksburg. . . . Troops could scarcely find dry ground on which to pitch their tents. Malarial fevers broke out among the men. Measles and small pox also attacked them. . . . Visitors to the camps went home with dismal stories to relate; Northern papers came back to the soldiers with these stories exaggerated.[1]

Widely criticized, Grant learned that he had to cultivate a thick skin in dealing with unwarranted attacks if he was to maintain leadership, promote unity in the ranks and ultimately attain victory. He learned to be receptive to input when it was appropriate (as with the news from Ms. Livermore) and to ignore disparaging remarks he knew were wrong (the sensational newspaper accounts).

> It takes great humility to own up to mistakes when we've made them and graciously disregard those errors that aren't really ours.

It takes a truly wise and fair-minded person to discern the difference between justified and unjustified criticism. And it takes great humility to own up to mistakes when we've made them and graciously disregard those errors that aren't really ours. These are indeed the kinds of qualities—wisdom, fairness and humility—we all need to navigate the muddy terrain of relationships today. In our culture, we find ourselves dealing with increasingly complex and high-stress issues: managing in-law relationships, blended families, single parenting and relationship restoration. In the following pages, I want to give some practical tips for families struggling with these four areas.

IN-LAWS

I have met many in-laws who acted like outlaws; that is, they felt as though they could break the rules of relationships. They brought pressure unintentionally into their children's homes and families. One of the primary ways that in-laws become outlaws is that they command an unhealthy amount of influence and freely dispense advice and criticism. They manipulate and intrude instead of allowing their kids to live their own lives.

The Bible provides some guidelines for dealing with these delicate situations. We are told, "'Honor your father and mother'—which is the first commandment with a promise—'that it may go well with you and that you may enjoy long life on the earth'" (Eph. 6:2-3). I believe this applies to parents by marriage as well as our own moms and dads. Therefore, honor and respect must underlie all of our interactions with in-laws. And this must be balanced with another biblical principle: "A man will leave his father and mother and be united to his wife, and they will become one flesh" (Gen. 2:24). The Hebrew word for "leave" has the connotation of loosening. We never fully leave our families; we simply loosen the bonds. The loosening of the parental bonds allows us to develop intimacy and closeness with our spouse and children. We are to create our own families, apart from our parents.

So how do we comply with both of these biblical injunctions—maintaining honor for our parents while separating from them? The answer lies in creating healthy boundaries. In many in-law relationships, trust and respect are violated. Couples feel as though Mom, Dad or other relatives have a specific agenda to promote and, because they are younger than their parents and other in-laws, their opinions and wishes don't matter. These couples—in love and grace—must hold firm limits with parents and in-laws (more on boundaries in a moment).

Although there are many aspects of in-law problems, I want to address three common ones.

Mama's-Boy and Daddy's-Girl Syndrome

A mama's boy is a young man who has an unusually close identification and communication style with his mother. And, of course, the same is true for girls and their dads (hereafter I'll refer only to males, but the principles are generally the same for both genders). Often this young man was able to avoid or get around the desires of his dad by simply going to mama. In the realm of single parenting, it may also mean that Dad was never around, which caused the bond between mom and son to grow stronger.

In some cases, there may have been transgressions of normal boundaries of a parent-child relationship. Mama became unusually close emotionally, acting more like a lover or girlfriend than a parent. Therefore, she has shared intimate concerns about her life with her son. The son has grown up with the idea that he is an emotional guardian responsible for protecting his mother. If that emotional duty has been established and a wife enters into the relationship, major clashes are likely to ensue.

Jacob is the classic mama's boy of the Scriptures. In Genesis 27, we read that Rebecca teaches her son how to lie and manipulate for a "good cause" (see vv. 10-20). Although Jacob may have been robust and masculine, he handled conflict in a scheming, manipulative way. For example, when he ran away from Laban's house, he dealt with his unfair compensation in a conniving way. And although God told Jacob to leave his father-in-law's house, he did not obey the Lord in an ethical way. Moreover, Jacob deceived Laban by not telling him he was running away (see Gen. 31).

A woman who marries into a mama's-boy situation may feel like an intruder. Her mother-in-law views her as a threat and perhaps an adversary. Sometimes mothers of mama's boys will openly criticize their new daughter-in-law. In the guise of fulfilling their parental duty, they *help* their new daughter take care of *their* baby. This leads to manipulation, guilt trips, fear and pressure within the marriage. Daughters-in-law in this situation should avoid falling into three major pitfalls:

1. thinking that she is going to change this relationship overnight;

2. verbally attacking the mother-in-law (you can't win!);
3. trying too hard to win the mother's approval.

Often this type of mother will never be fully satisfied with her daughter-in-law. Many wives, in an attempt to gain the respect of a mother-in-law, go out of their way to try to make this woman love them. The wife will cook and clean tirelessly yet also allow her husband's mom to interrupt the family at inappropriate times. Trying to earn love is a trap that will eventually lead to feeling hurt and disrespected. There may also be long-term damage to her marriage because of the resentment that trying too hard to please Mom can bring.

Financial Dependence
Only in rare cases does money given or loaned to family members not come with strings attached. Parents and in-laws who give their kids money often feel that they have the right to dispense advice and influence decisions. They want to be informed and updated on all the goings-on. After all, they figure they're funding what is being done.

I've known many young couples who have received loans from parents or lived with Mom and Dad for whatever reason. Working in the family business can also bring a couple into financial dependence. If you are in one of these situations, I encourage you to follow these three principles.

1. If you are living in the home of a family member, submit to the house rules. Make sure you don't violate anything that is a high priority for the host family.
2. If you are working for a family-owned company, never allow familial relationships to cause you to challenge and disrespect the rules of the business.
3. If you are in a family business, create a financial war

chest so you will be able to move on and become independent if things get sticky.

Elderly Parents

Because people are living longer these days, parents and in-laws often become dependent on the care of their children. On this issue, the Bible's instruction is perfectly clear.

If anyone does not provide for his relatives, and especially for his immediate family, he has denied the faith and is worse than an unbeliever (1 Tim. 5:8).

Though it's clear from Paul's teaching to Timothy that believers should care for their family members, the specifics are left for us to discern. How much financial support do we give elderly parents? Do we invite them to live under our roof? Do we spend time caring for parents when it drains time from our immediate family? All of these issues, and dozens more, can cause conflict between husband and wife.

I believe the majority of Christians would gladly sacrifice a bit of their lifestyle to make elderly parents and in-laws more comfortable. But it sometimes takes the wisdom of Solomon to maintain a healthy balance. Imagine having to choose between medicine for your mother and shoes for your child. Should a gifted child be denied private schooling because his grandmother requires specialized care or a residential home? Only you can make these decisions, but each will have to be addressed. It would be better to talk about these things *before* your mom and dad become ill, grow older or begin to have physical problems. As the saying goes, I believe you should talk about how you will act in times of war during the seasons of peace.

Healthy Boundaries

As you deal with a healthy solution to the issues described above, at least two problems are likely to emerge. The first is external—the anger of others. Many people are intimidated by the threat of an angry response from their in-laws. Sometimes the in-laws move into "guilt projection," which has its roots in anger. By guilt projection, I mean family members telling you how poorly you handle things and trying to make you feel guilty. Statements like: "You don't care about me" or "You weren't there when I needed you" can cause us to feel that our limits are too rigid or even motivated by selfishness. In *Boundaries*, Drs. Henry Cloud and John Townsend say, "The angry person has a character problem. If you reinforce this character problem, it will return tomorrow. And the next day in other situations."[2]

The second problem with boundaries is an internal problem—the fear of anger. This is part of what the Bible means when it refers to the "fear of man" (Prov. 29:25). Sometimes when I take a bold step to confront someone, my concern about the person's reaction makes me feel tense. This can be so overwhelming that I refuse to bring up the offenses that are hindering the relationship.

In those instances, pray about the relationship with your in-laws, believing that God will enable you to establish healthy boundaries. These may include making sure that both sets of parents are equally cared for or setting limits on how much input they're allowed to give on your decisions. Using the communication keys I have shared in earlier chapters, talk with your spouse about boundaries as early as you can. Do not hesitate to seek counseling for these issues so they don't divide your marriage.

BLENDED FAMILIES

Because of the high divorce rate in America, blended families are now commonplace. And given that these families come in all shapes, sizes and ages, there is not a one-size-fits-all template for how to behave. Rather, every person involved—moms, dads, kids, even grandparents and cousins—will have to adjust and bend to the challenges of the unique situation. Relationships must be negotiated and compromises made if harmony is going to prevail. Sound tiring and taxing? That's because it is.

Remember, family intimacy and connectedness don't *just happen*. Relational rules are hammered out and agreed upon by those involved. You have to decide specifically what areas need to be agreed upon. Several issues can be sources of confusion and conflict if not handled properly. Let's look at five areas about which parents of blended families must be especially vigilant.

Sexual-Romantic Boundaries

Many spouses in blended families live with an unspoken insecurity about previous relationships. After all, former couples were attracted to each other enough to marry. Many fear that the adage Absence makes the heart grow fonder just might come true. Some new spouses may wonder if there's lingering sexual attraction for the ex-husband or ex-wife.

Guard your heart and your body at all costs! If you have remarried and your ex-spouse has not, there very well could be leftover attraction. No matter how devastating the breakup was, close proximity could rekindle romantic feelings. Pray for God's help to keep your thoughts pure and your actions above reproach.

Respect for Ex-Mates

In a world where wars within broken families are anything but civil, there is still a need for civility, courtesy and respect. Your children need a sense of security and fairness that can only come from their parents, even when they're no longer married. When parents verbally attack each other's character, children naturally become defensive.

Your ex-mate may have been a horrible spouse, and you may be justified in avoiding him or her. In fact, you may end up in arguments sometimes, but do so in private. At least make an agreement not to criticize or belittle each other in front of the children. A divorce or separation is not the children's fault, although they often feel that it is. Therefore, you owe them all of the security and emotional safety you can provide. Much of this is achieved by treating your ex-spouse with decency and decorum.

Authority Within New Family Structures

In blended families, matters of authority and rule making often get complicated. Kids are left to wonder, *Who's in charge here? My dad, stepdad, mom, stepmom?* It can be perplexing for kids and adolescents.

In the typical blended family, the household that used to be one unit is now at least two. If this is the case, we can't talk about the rules of the other house as though they don't matter. The authority of each household must be respected. We can't chip away at the credibility of the other family and what they are doing there. This will only breed rebellion in our own children. What we can do is share our own standards and what we want in our homes. But we can't do it at the expense of the other home.

If our children ask which set of rules is right, we can simply say that there are different ways to approach life (so long as nothing dishonest or immoral is going on). If, in fact, your ex-spouse is definitely wrong or is being neglectful in some way, it would probably be best to have a qualified third-party look into the situation. On the other hand, you can't afford to hurt your children by attacking your mate merely because you disagree about how his or her household is run.

Children's Emotional Security

If you are the primary caregiver of a child and your family has gone through a divorce, it would be obvious that you need to be available to your child by spending time listening and caring. Those who only have children on a visitation basis may not recognize that the kids need, above all, a sense of support rather than feeling like a pawn on a chessboard.

If you are not the custodial caregiver, and you receive your child as infrequently as once a week or once every month, your role should also be to listen and spend time with them. Your biological children need to sense your genuine care without trying to change the structures of their home and school.

Many divorced or separated people do not fully comprehend the impact their presence has on their kids. Therefore, they may become a little lax in planning time with the child. Other parents become distant from their children because they have problems with their ex-spouse. They stay away because they tire of the drama. In both cases, the child feels abandoned. He or she didn't ask to be part of a broken home.

The Stepparent's Important Role

The role of a stepparent is ill-defined at best. The Bible has a special category for this role—it's called parent. The only difference between parenting and stepparenting is that the latter requires the permission of two people—the spouse and the child. Respect must be earned and trust built.

I encourage stepparents to serve their spouse's children in love. It takes a special grace to love someone else's kids. It would be difficult at best to raise someone else's children unless you understand and value the parent's approach. For the average blended family, this will take a lot of talking, planning and prayer.

SINGLE PARENTING

The number of single parents in America is growing at an alarming rate. Among the black community, 70 percent of children

will soon be in a family that has only one parent.[3] American society in general seems to be following that same tragic pattern.
Indeed, this is an overwhelming problem for our culture. God
intended children to receive the nurture and influence of both a
mom and a dad. Without the consistent guidance of one or the
other, kids grow up with a void, an empty place in their hearts.

Most single parents in America are women. Although a
growing number of men are attempting to provide for a family
by themselves, there is still a tendency for society to applaud the
courageous efforts of a woman who has been divorced, widowed,
abandoned or never married. Women responsible for shaping
the lives of a future generation often have overwhelming feelings
of being alone, and they are in desperate need of support and
help. Our society is learning to respond to what seems to be the
disintegration of the nuclear family, but we've got a long way to
go to address this crisis.

Although I can't possibly cover all the complexities of single
parenting, let me offer four principles for you to consider. I'll
address them to women, but they apply to fathers as well.

Recognize That You Cannot Function as Both Parents

If you are a woman, you cannot be a dad physically, emotionally
or spiritually. Don't put yourself under the pressure of having to
make up for the missing father. This simply won't happen,
because it can't happen. Even the parents of an intact biological
family cannot meet all of a child's needs. This is why we must
place our children in God's hands and trust Him to supply the
needs that we can't.

Every mother has access to the same spiritual resources that
parents of intact homes have. In the busyness of our society, biological fathers are often absent from home simply because of the
demands of making a living. His input is often symbolic and
ceremonial, yet in Christian homes we understand that his role

represents to a great measure the authority of God. There are five things that fathers are supposed to bring to a home:

- Affection
- Affirmation
- Authority
- Appreciation
- Acceptance

Ultimately, God Himself provides each one of these things for us. When a father is not available, God will move to meet that child and to reveal Himself in other ways. Most of our earthly fathers were deficient in one or more of these areas. If there is a measure of wholeness in our lives, it is because our heavenly Father has stepped in.

Solicit Mentors

Mentors are important for all children and absolutely critical for those from single-parent homes. If these kids have someone to talk to other than the single parent, it will increase sensitivity to the consequences of many of their actions. Consider these statistics.

- Most teens—81 percent—feel that talking with an adult helps to reduce the risk of pregnancy.
- Most students—53 percent—credit mentors with improving their ability to avoid drugs.
- Most young people—59 percent—improved their grades while they were being mentored.
- Most children in community-based mentoring pro-grams—96 percent—stayed in school.[4]

We hear statistics like these, and we respond by desiring to find a "master mentor." This is a superhero of our imagination with so much love that he takes the place of a dad. Remember, I said that a single female parent couldn't assume the role of a dad; neither can this master mentor. The apostle Paul said, "Even though you have ten thousand guardians in Christ, you do not have many fathers" (1 Cor. 4:15). Guardians and teachers can pass on values and skills, but only for a season and in limited scope. Children need many different kinds of mentors to substitute for the father who isn't there.

Screening the men who will be closely involved with your children is very significant. Make sure that there are physical boundaries in place in order to prevent physical or emotional abuse. Let me mention five kinds of mentors you should consider.

- *An academic mentor or consistent tutor.* If monitored, the relationship will bring out positive relational skills as well as academic improvement.
- *A coach or instructor in a particular skill.* When you have identified an area of giftedness in your child (art, athletics, drama or the like), find a mentor who can cultivate that skill.
- *A career mentor.* As children reach the teen years, they need to begin thinking about a vocation. There is no hurry to make definite decisions, but your child will benefit from meeting with someone of the same sex who can model how to pursue your child's dreams.
- *A lifestyle or life mentor.* This is a general mentor who is available to talk with your child about anything and everything. This person is simply to be a positive influence on your child's life. Perhaps there is someone you know at your church who would serve in this capacity. Another good resource is the Big Brothers and Big Sisters of America.

- *A spiritual mentor.* A youth pastor or one of the workers in your church's youth department would be a great mentor to disciple your child in spiritual disciplines.

If you can only find one mentor initially, that's okay. It's a start. But ideally, kids from single-parent homes need four to five people with varying skills. If each of them meets with your child just once or twice a month, you'll find that their input and positive modeling will be a great influence.

Don't Date

I may receive some debate about this point, but I believe a single parent should not date until her child leaves home. The reason is: Different men coming in and out of the house will have a potential for negative relational bonding with the child. On-again, off-again relationships will only tarnish your child's view of love, romance and marriage. However, if you do decide to date, do not bring them to your home or discuss them incessantly. You know how it is—we often think relationships are going somewhere before we hit the proverbial bump in the road. If you set up expectations about a new stepdad, the fallout can be devastating for your child should the relationship falter.

Plan Sabbaths

God had a terrific idea when He decided that one day a week should be set aside for rest. Unfortunately, for most people—especially single parents—this sounds more like a pipe dream than a practical proposal.

If you are the single breadwinner in your family, you will most likely be stressed and overworked much of the time. I encourage you to begin planning a regular sabbatical in your schedule. If it is not feasible to do this once a week, then plan for once a month or even once every other month.

As a single parent, you may need to have seasonal rest breaks. Perhaps once every quarter you can get away for a weekend. These breaks will allow you to get a deep rest and a break from constant demands. When you return to the enormously important duties, you will come back with renewed energy.

RELATIONSHIP RESTORATION

Marriages break down for many reasons—inability to talk openly, anger mismanagement, overwork and on and on. The principles I shared in previous chapters, particularly the ones covering communication and conflict resolution, will apply to a variety of difficult situations.

One problem that has brought dozens of couples to my office for counseling over the past 10 years is infidelity. Men and women often justify infidelity by focusing on unmet needs. The type of people they cheat with often differ drastically from their spouse. Let me make some general—and generally true—statements that explain why it takes so much effort to rekindle the passion in a marriage relationship.

- One difference is that a man is looking for a playmate, while the woman is looking for a soul mate.
- A husband thinks a sexual affair is really nothing, involving his body only, but a wife will get involved because she connected emotionally.
- He needs someone to talk to; she needs someone to listen.

If you're concerned that your spouse might fall into infidelity, find out what he or she is yearning for. If your spouse has been unfaithful, find out why he or she strayed. It's often a combination of little things with a massive dose of poor judgment that leads to marital transgression. We are often filled with self-doubt at these moments. We imagine competitors with allure and sexual prowess that would make us look like pygmies in the land of the giants. We can feel pressured or hopeless. Take heart. If you can identify problems and create a strategy that meets the need, the relationship can be restored.

Many people advocate temporary separations as a way to cure family ills, whether they be related to infidelity or other significant problems. Though this may be an effective strategy in exceptional cases, this is tantamount to taking an invasive action in surgery. Healing may result, but high risks are involved. Recent statistics show that 75 percent of couples who separate end up divorced within two years, and 90 percent divorce within five years.[5] My feeling is that married couples should separate only under extreme conditions (such as when domestic abuse is involved) and within carefully monitored parameters (such as where each spouse will live, how much contact they will have and how long they will live apart). This should be done under the guidance of a trusted counselor or pastor.

Fixing a broken relationship is one of the most difficult things to do in life. The major reason for this is that it takes a tremendous amount of time and energy. We are willing to invest much in new relationships because of the emotional payoff that dreams and romance give us. The problem with the existing relationship is that it is already flawed, already timeworn, already mundane. James Dobson sums it up nicely:

> We crave that which we can't attain, but we disrespect that which we can't escape. This axiom is particularly relevant in romantic matters, and has probably influenced your love life. Now the forgotten part of this characteristic is that marriage does not erase or change it. Whenever one marriage partner grovels in his own

disrespect . . . when he reveals his fear of rejection by the mate . . . when he begs and pleads for a handout . . . he often faces a bewildering attitude of disdain from the one he needs and loves. Just as in the premarital relationship, nothing douses more water on a romantic flame than for one partner to fling himself emotionally on the other, accepting disrespect in stride. He says in effect, "No matter how badly you treat me, I'll still be here at your feet, because I can't survive without you." This is the best way I know to kill a beautiful friendship.[6]

> # Restoring damaged relationships takes courage, inner strength and self respect.

Restoring damaged relationships takes courage, inner strength and self-respect. We must be brave enough to confront problems, no matter how painful. We also have to make an unwavering commitment to the regeneration of the relationship. We often begin the reconciliation process with a combination of optimism and apprehension, and sometimes we're less committed to a process than we should be. We must become convinced that God has the power to heal any broken relationship. Then we can say with the biblical writers:

> The Spirit of the LORD will rest on him—the Spirit of wisdom and of understanding, the Spirit of counsel and of power (Isa. 11:2).

> The God of hope [will] fill you with all joy and peace as you trust in him, so that you may overflow with hope by the power of the Holy Spirit (Rom. 15:13).

The power of God will come into play if you truly decide to work on your relationship. Though your problems may be daunting, you have the creator of the universe walking with you through the restoration process. God strongly desires for your marriage to be healed, and He stands ready to supply all the power to make that happen.

CHRIST-CENTERED

There are moments in our lives when we find ourselves camped out at a place similar to where Grant was in his campaign against Vicksburg. We can be in the dead of winter waiting for a transition to spring, unable to move forward. At times like this, we are most often criticized by people who don't understand what we are trying to do. We can be distracted from taking action that could really change our locale. In order to ensure that you are poised for change, reevaluate your paradigms and work at what you need to improve your family life.

No individual can give you all the remedies to your problems. We ultimately have to depend on Christ, and He will lead us to the counselors, resources and circumstances that will give us understanding in our challenging relationships. God will help us negotiate our lives so that we may move into the new dimension that He has ordained.

EPILOGUE

Out of the Jungle

Success is how high you bounce when you hit bottom.

General George S. Patton, during World War II

I began this book by telling you the story of the War of the Roses, and you may recall that this conflict began as a family feud. A family that should have led a nation to peace became an example of treachery, infidelity and an insatiable hunger for power.

An American proverb states, "A great war leaves the country with three armies: an army of cripples, an army of mourners, and an army of thieves."[1] This is true with family wars as well as national wars. Generations of our family's sons and daughters will be crippled emotionally because of family war. Their scarred psyches often negatively impact their descendants. This was the case with the royal family of England.

If there ever was a dysfunctional family, the descendants of Edward III were a classic example. Every negative aspect of relational life discussed in this book was lived out on one or both sides of that influential family.

The world would have been different if this royal family could have taken the understanding of Christ and Christianity from *head* knowledge and made it *heart* knowledge. If they could have lived out what they said with their mouths, their legacy would have been extremely different. Remember, these were the descendants of the crusaders, whose aim was to protect the Christian faith.

I have purposely given you a great deal of information and practical suggestions in this book. Knowledge is power, as the folk proverb says. Knowledge also brings awareness and a sense of responsibility. Once we realize that things need to change and that we are responsible, a kind of "spiritual indigestion" may come upon us. Like Ezekiel in the Old Testament, we have eaten the scroll. It is sweet to the taste but bitter in our bellies. Perhaps you are asking yourself, *What do I do now? How do I bring real resolution to my family problems and not let them linger on indefinitely? If one of the richest families in history could not solve their problems, how can I put things back together? Harry and Michele Jackson can't come and give me personal counsel, so what do I do now?*

The answer is deceptively simple: Start where you are. Decide to improve your life and serve your family with excellence. One of the best secretaries that I ever had would recite the following phrase whenever she felt overwhelmed: "How do you eat an elephant? One bite at a time!"

There's your answer. Break down your daunting problem into bite-sized pieces.

This means you have to set some priorities. Begin with small problems in order to build your confidence, and then launch into the areas that really concern you. The Holy Spirit will guide you in this process.

In chapter one, I told you about a time I got lost driving to a radio station in Northern Virginia in the dead of night. It was a trip I had taken many times during the bright sunshine of day, but that time I traveled a familiar road without the sun to illuminate the road ahead. Similarly, there are many of us who know a lot about marriage and family life, but we will never be able to find our real destination unless the light of the Son of God is shining upon us. We must discover that the sun is the light of God's Word; it is personal communion with Him.

I trust, as you close this book, you will be so gripped with the power and love of God that you will desire to bring forth revelations of the glory of Christ. I pray that it will be said of you that you battled for your family in the name of Jesus. I hope that instead of the War of the Roses, you will lift up the Rose of Sharon and His mighty power.

It's a jungle out there, but you can make it!

ENDNOTES

Chapter 1

1. John Julius Norwich, *Shakespeare's Kings* (New York: Touchstone, 1999), p. 16.
2. U.S. Census Bureau, "Index of/population/socdemo/marr-div/," *Census Bureau Home Page,* 2002. http://www.census.gov/population/socdemo/marr-div/ (accessed April 2002).
3. Ibid.
4. David Popenoe, Ph.D., "National Marriage Project, Rutgers University," *Rutgers University Home Page,* 2002. http://www.rutgers.edu (accessed April 2002).
5. George Barna, "Christians Are More Likely to Experience Divorce Than Are Non-Christians," *Barna Research Group, Ltd.,* 1999. http://www.barna.org (accessed April 2002).
6. *Merriam-Webster's Collegiate Dictionary*, 10th ed., s.v. "radical."
7. Cecil Maranville, "Divorce Revolution Spawns the Cohabitation Generation," *United Church of God Home Page,* 2000. http://www.ucg.org/articles/gn/cohabita.html (accessed April 2002).
8. J. Allan Petersen, ed., *The Marriage Affair, The Family Counselor* (Wheaton, IL: Tyndale House Publishers, 1989), p. 2.
9. Ibid.
10. The Los Angeles-based Bloods and Crips are probably the most widely recognized gangs in America due to their media exposure received in the 1980s. These groups have migrated throughout the country and are seen in most states and their prison populations. There are literally hundreds of sets or individual gangs under the Blood and Crip names. They are no longer racially specific.
11. Petersen, ed., *The Marriage Affair, The Family Counselor*, p. 3.
12. Ibid., p. 5.

Chapter 2

1. Mark Water, ed., *The New Encyclopedia of Christian Quotations* (Grand Rapids, MI: Baker Books, 2000), p. 168.
2. William Shakespeare, *Hamlet*, 3.1.57-61.
3. Neil Clark Warren, *Finding the Love of Your Life* (Colorado Springs, CO: Focus on the Family, 1992), pp. 66-67.

Chapter 3

1. Kenneth L. Woodward, "Sex, Morality and the Protestant Ministry: What Sexual Standards Should Clergy Obey?" *Newsweek* (July 28, 2001), p. 62.

2. "Fundamental Baptist Information Service," *Way of Life Literature Home Page,* 2002. http://www.wayoflife.org (accessed April 2002).

3. Robert G. Torricelli, ed., *Quotations for Public Speakers: A Historical, Literary, and Political Anthology* (New Brunswick, NJ: Rutgers University Press, 2001), p. 248.

4. Michael Baisden, *Never Satisfied: How and Why Men Cheat* (Katy, TX: Legacy Publishing, 1995), p. 127.

5. John Gray, Ph.D., *Men, Women and Relationships* (New York: HarperCollins Publishers, 1993), p. 17.

6. Gary Chapman, *The Five Love Languages* (Chicago, IL: Northfield Publishing, 1995), n.p.

7. Phillip C. McGraw, *Relationship Rescue* (New York: Hyperion, 2000), p. 56.

Chapter 4

1. Mark Water, ed., *The New Encyclopedia of Christian Quotations* (Grand Rapids, MI: Baker Books, 2000), p. 695.

2. Stephen Covey, *The Seven Habits of Highly Effective People* (New York: Fireside Books, 1989), p. 98.

3. Ibid.

4. Water, ed., *The New Encyclopedia of Christian Quotations,* p. 404.

5. An example of this can be found in the values of Arthur Andersen, the accounting firm whose reputation was damaged by the Enron scandal. A statement of their values appears at http://www.andersen.com (accessed April 2002) and reads as follows: "We believe in integrity and respect. We believe in maintaining a passion for excellence in people, service and innovation. And we believe in demonstrating a commitment to personal growth through training and development." Although the majority of the employees of this firm held to these high standards, a few select persons have blackened their corporate eye. They lost the vision and values set before them.

6. Charles Handy, *The Age of Paradox* (Boston, MA: Harvard Business School, 1994), p. 50, quoted in Robert P. Buford, *Half Time* (New York: HarperCollins, 1994), p. 107.

Chapter 5

1. "America's National Parks Store," *America's National Parks Home Page,* 2002. http://www.eparks.com (accessed April 2002).

2. Robert G. Torricelli, ed., *Quotations for Public Speakers: A Historical, Literary, and Political Anthology* (New Brunswick, NJ: Rutgers University Press, 2001), p. 47.

3. John Bartlett and Justin Kaplan, eds., *Bartlett's Familiar Quoatations* (New York: Little, Brown and Company, 1992), p. 572.

4. John Gray, *Men, Women and Relationships* (New York: HarperCollins Publishers, 1993), p. 280.

5. H. Norman Wright, *Communication at Work* (Ventura, CA: Regal Books, 2001), p. 150.

Chapter 6

1. Eugene Ehrlich and Marshall DeBruhl, comps., *The International Thesaurus of Quotations* (New York: HarperCollins Publishers, 1996), p. 412.
2. Peggy Anderson, comp., *Great Quotes from Great Women* (Franklin Lakes, NJ: Career Press, 1997), p. 77.
3. Richard Brooks, ed., *Atlas of World History* (New York: HarperCollins Publishers, 2000), p. 22.

Chapter 7

1. Stephen E. Ambrose, *The Victors* (New York: Simon and Schuster, 1989), p. 189.
2. *Merriam-Webster's Collegiate Dictionary*, 10th ed., s.v. "grace."
3. *Strong's Exhaustive Concordance*, s.v. "grace."
4. Robert G. Torricelli, ed., *Quotations for Public Speakers: A Historical, Literary, and Political Anthology* (New Brunswick, NJ: Rutgers University Press, 2001), p. 82.
5. Douglas Carlton Abrams, "Father Nature: The Making of a Modern Dad," *Psychology Today,* April 2002, p. 40.
6. Lynn Ponton, M.D., *The Sex Lives of Teenagers* (New York: Penguin Putnam, 2000), p. 257.

Chapter 8

1. Ehrlich and DeBruhl, comps., *The International Thesaurus of Quotations*, p. 626.
2. George Barna, *The Future of the American Family* (Chicago, IL: Moody Press, 1993), p. 129.
3. Ibid.
4. Robert J. Morgan, ed., *Nelson's Complete Book of Stories, Illustrations and Quotes* (Nashville, TN: Thomas Nelson, 2000), p. 529.
5. Steven Simring, M.D. and Sue Klavans Simring, D.S.W., *Making Marriages Work for Dummies* (New York: IDG Books Worldwide, 1999), p. 231.
6. Ed Wheat, M.D. and Gayle Wheat, *Intended for Pleasure* (Grand Rapids, MI: Fleming H. Revell, 1977), p. 223.
7. Ibid.
8. Dr. Willard F. Harley, Jr. and Dr. Jennifer Harley Chalmers, *Surviving an Affair* (Grand Rapids, MI: Fleming H. Revell, 1998), p. 139.

Chapter 9

1. Helen Kooiman Hosier, *100 Christian Women Who Changed the Twentieth Century* (Grand Rapids, MI: Fleming H. Revell, 2000), p. 229.
2. Larry Burkett, *Personal Finances* (Chicago: Moody Press, 1991), p. 61.

3. Florence Nightingale Museum, "Resource Centre and Research Papers," *Florence Nightingale Museum Home Page,* 2002. http://www.florence-nightingale.co.uk/ (accessed April 2002).

4. Larry Burkett, *The Family Financial Workbook* (Chicago: Moody Press, 2000); Ron Blue, *Taming the Money Monster* (Colorado Springs, CO: Focus on the Family, 2000); Mary Hunt, *Debt-Proof Living* (Nashville, TN: Broadman and Holman Publishers, 1999).

5. Barbara Loos, *I Haven't Saved a Dime, Now What?!* (New York: Silver Lining Books, 2000), p. 75.

Chapter 10

1. Al Kaltman, *Cigars, Whiskey and Winning* (Paramus, NJ: Prentice Hall, 1998), p. 116.

2. Dr. Henry Cloud and Dr. John Townsend, *Boundaries* (Grand Rapids, MI: Zondervan, 1992), p. 241.

3. California Mentor Foundation, "Big Brothers/Big Sisters," *California Mentor Foundation Home Page,* 2002. http://www.bbbsa.org and http://www.calmentor.com (accessed April 2002).

4. Ibid.

5. Ibid.

6. James Dobson, *What Wives Wish Their Husbands Knew About Women* (Wheaton, IL: Tyndale House Publishers, 1975), pp. 78-84.

Epilogue

1. Peter G. Tsouras, ed., *The Greenhill Dictionary of Military Quotations* (London: Greenhill Books, 2000), p. 525.

Become an Overcomer

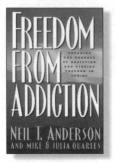

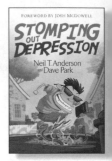

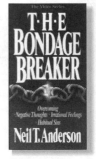

job #043754

Learn to Live Happily with Your Spouse, Kids and God

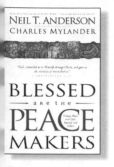

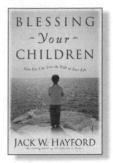

Blessed Are the Peacemakers
Finding Peace with God, Yourself and Others
Neil T. Anderson and Charles Mylander
Paperback • ISBN 08307.28910

The Marriage Checkup
How Healthy Is Your Marriage?
Dr. H. Norman Wright
Paperback • ISBN 08307.30699

Blessing Your Children
How You Can Love the Kids in Your Life
Jack W. Hayford
Gift Hardcover • ISBN 08307.30796

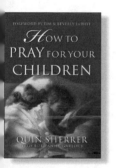

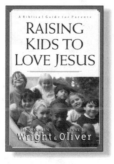

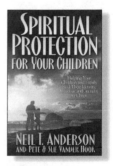

How to Pray for Your Children
Foreword by Tim and Beverly LaHaye
Quin Sherrer and Ruthanne Garlock
Paperback • ISBN 08307.22017

Raising Kids to Love Jesus
A Biblical Guide for Parents
H. Norman Wright and Gary J. Oliver
Paperback • ISBN 08307.21533

Spiritual Protection for Your Children
Helping Your Children Find Their Identity, Security and Freedom in Christ
Neil T. Anderson and Pete and Sue Vander Hook
Paperback • ISBN 08307.18869

job #043754